Mary McAdams
Personal Copy

THE
WORTH
ETHIC

THE
WORTH
ETHIC

HOW TO PROFIT FROM THE CHANGING VALUES OF THE NEW WORK FORCE

KATE LUDEMAN, Ph.D.

E. P. DUTTON ✍ NEW YORK

Published in the United States by E. P. Dutton,
a division of NAL Penguin Inc.,
2 Park Avenue, New York, N.Y. 10016.

Published simultaneously in Canada by Fitzhenry and Whiteside, Limited,
Toronto.

Library of Congress Cataloging-in-Publication Data

Ludeman, Kate.
    The worth ethic : how to profit from the changing values
of the new work force / Kate Ludeman.—1st ed.
        p.   cm.
    ISBN 0-525-24756-4
    1. Work ethic—Case studies.   2. KLA Instruments—Case studies.
3. Human capital—Case studies.   I. Title.
        HD4905.L84   1990   88-28512
            658.3′14—dc19   CIP

Designed by Margo D. Barooshian

1   3   5   7   9   10   8   6   4   2

First Edition

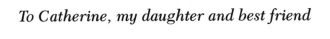

To Catherine, my daughter and best friend

CONTENTS

ACKNOWLEDGMENTS

I didn't invent the Worth Ethic. I was raised with it. For my first experiences with the powers of self-worth and caring, I thank my parents. Their steadiness and affection gave me the emotional freedom to ask weird questions, argue, and talk back. We didn't know until much later that this was not common in our generation. To this day, my brother Ben, my sister Debi, and I seek each other's company and counsel when life gets especially tough or extremely special. My mother virtually defined the quantum jump for me by becoming a published author and historian in her middle years, when she faced an empty nest. My father taught me the joy of work. He encouraged me to be feminine and to speak my mind, making it clear I didn't have to choose one over the other. My extended family—the Ludemans, Kimballs, and especially my Martin grandparents, aunts, uncles and cousins—taught me that people are living, breathing, and needful, not indifferent objects. My Aunt Helen Ludeman, a professional with a doctorate in chemistry (from back in 1920) showed me that a woman can have power and influence outside the home. I owe very special thanks to my daughter, Catherine. Articulate, introspective, and loving beyond anything I could have hoped for in a daughter, she survived the tough early years and infuses joy in my life.

So many superb people helped me see my potential and reach out for it. Gay Hendricks believed I had something worth writing about. He helped me break down the psychotherapeutic process into the CHANGING Process's eight steps. Without his encouragement the manuscript would still be a glimmer of insight locked away in my heart. Bob Ray gave me the boost that carried me successfully from engineering to psychology, and John Enright led me through important, early leaps of personal development. LaUna Huffines acted first as a guide, and then later as a friend, showing me the very real power of love in the work world. Gary Berger took a chance on me, gave me my first management job, and taught me the corporate ropes. Jack Hart gave me a vision of human resources and taught me much about balancing business objectives with people's needs.

All the people at KLA, a composite of hundreds, touched my life in significant ways they may not even realize. I am especially grateful for the caring support of Bob Riopel, to whom I reported when I began this book. I also wish to thank my staff, who proved that the Worth Ethic works. Our relationships have deepened to friendship over the years, and they consistently surpass all my expectations.

Joani Selement, who edited my manuscript, time and again put a name to the ideas I was writing about and helped me to frame the final focus of the book. Pat Anderson, my wonderful and faithful assistant, invested many long hours of extra effort and special care to ready the manuscript. Sandy Dijkstra, my literary agent, recognized the value of the Worth Ethic and shared generously her extensive knowledge of the book business. Dick Marek, Amy Mintzer, Jean Rawitt, and all the other people at Dutton brought the book to life and helped me get it in the hands of people who would benefit from it.

I deeply appreciate the difference each one of you made in my life.

INTRODUCTION

Love is the most powerful force in the world, and that includes the world of work. For a long time I hesitated to say that aloud. I am, after all, an engineer, psychologist, corporate executive, and management consultant. In those roles my ultimate goals are productivity and profit. Without these goals we wouldn't have a workplace. Yet, you can't run a company on brain power and muscle power alone. You need the human heart at work.

Nobody talks much about "love" at work. It's as taboo as sex was twenty years ago. Love and sex are so closely linked in contemporary culture, we've almost forgotten the deeper meanings of love. Yes, we approve of open communication and honest disagreement between employee and boss, but that's as close as we come to encouraging a free exchange of feelings in the office, shop, company halls, or parking lot. We act as if somehow we would doom our business to failure if we once admitted that we love our work team for its skilled performances, love our products for their genuine usefulness, or love our managers for the productivity they inspire. The opposite is true.

Early on, I knew I wanted to help people find more meaning and satisfaction in what they did in life. After graduating from college, I spent a year in Vietnam working on a project I'd hoped would help the peasants displaced by the war. Disillusioned by my manager's focus on immediate politics rather than long-term social results, I returned to the U.S. to help college students and social service workers. Sadly, my efforts seemed to have little impact on the lives of the people I tried to help.

To achieve the broad impact I yearned for, I knew I would have to return to the business world that shapes our lives in so many ways. I found a position as a manager of training and development for a large manufacturing company, where I encountered great numbers of people who functioned mainly with their thinking sides. My first challenge was to enhance the quality of their lives by introducing them to the emotional and intuitive world I knew. But this time I was better prepared than I was in Saigon. When managers presented me with their "logical options" and "necessary actions," I countered with Nietzsche: "Necessity is not a fact, it's an interpretation." Naturally, my idealism didn't bear immediate fruit. Still, I persisted.

Meanwhile I kept busy, raising a daughter alone, far from my rural Texas hometown. During this time, I especially missed the heartfelt interest and the emotional encouragement of my family. I missed the praise that told me someone believed in me, the concern and interest in my daughter, the fun and warm laughter I'd come to expect from my dad, mom, sister, and brother. Then as the months and years passed, I found family substitutes, different people who filled these familial roles. That's when I noticed my own renewed enthusiasm for work whenever someone showed me an extra measure of personal support. And I noticed that many of the company's employees, like me, were divorced, single, or living far from their extended families. I wasn't alone—we all needed more heart in the workday.

In my job, my first efforts focused on training programs oriented toward strengthening people's communication skills. These programs clearly touched and moved participants. Yet I saw few of the new skills integrated into their relationships with customers and employees. On the other hand, I saw senior managers and high-potential middle managers make internal shifts that stayed in place. These permanent changes came because they met with a psychologist or human resources executive such as myself for four to eight hours a month over the period of a year or more. This process was far slower than a two-day training program, but it worked.

About this time, I interviewed with Ken Levy and Bob Anderson, the founders of KLA Instruments and a team with formidable balance: Ken Levy, KLA's president, is the charismatic leader of the company's innovative technologists. They work unstintingly with Levy, transforming the science of high-speed image processing into practical automated optical inspection systems, each one of which is the first available in the marketplace. Bob Anderson, chairman of the board, is a creative financial expert who knows the difference between penny-pinching and fair play. From the beginning, he insisted on an equal sharing of profits and pleasant working conditions throughout the company.

KLA was my perfect opportunity: an entrepreneurial company receptive to innovative ideas. In Silicon Valley, Hewlett-Packard had already paved the way by building a company based on respect for the individual employee. KLA offered the chance to commit myself to a similar environment. Two of its officers had even come from Hewlett-Packard. So here was a company headed by people who already agreed with me that a company, like a family, needs to provide people with ongoing daily support. At KLA I began to examine the relationship between caring and productivity and to notice very specifically just what worked. The concept of a Worth Ethic began to jell.

At KLA I saw senior managers—including the president and chairman of the board—go to lunch in the employee cafeteria, sit down, talk, and listen to hourly employees. I saw entry-level engineers prodded to do original thinking about product design and to speak out when they had an idea. I saw honesty start at the top with all-employee discussions of quarterly sales and profits, openly compared to targeted goals, whether the news was bad or good. I saw the hierarchy frequently bypassed. When people talked about "we" at KLA, they meant everybody, from the top of the company to the last-hired engineer to entry-level production employees.

I joined KLA in 1984 when it had 300 employees and revenues were at $35 million. By 1989, the company had grown to nearly 1,000 employees and generated $180 million in revenue. KLA dominates the world market for automatic optical systems that inspect and control the manufacture of silicon wafers and photomasks used to make semiconductors. After surveying 1,200 security analysts and market researchers, *Electronic Business* chose KLA as one of eight excellent companies in the electronic business, right alongside IBM, Hewlett-Packard, and Digital Equipment. Several KLA employees were included in *Science Digest* in a list of one hundred of the most innovative minds nationwide. During the semiconductor industry's worst slowdown ever, 1986–1987, the company remained among the top twenty most profitable companies in Silicon Valley. Doing well in tough times proved we were doing something right.

How did we cope with this kind of growth and success? How did we create the spirit necessary for all this to happen? In KLA's open, caring environment, I managed to introduce practical systems that meet genuine human needs. These systems work because they affirm, coach, and support the genuine worth of every person in the company. The success of the

systems, the environment, and KLA's products proves to me
that what I've come to call the Worth Ethic works.

What, exactly, is the Worth Ethic? The Worth Ethic is a
belief in your indelible self-worth and the fundamental and
potential worth of others. People who live by the Worth Ethic
don't follow directions without thought or interest. Worth
Ethic employees take responsibility at work and put forth their
best efforts. Worth Ethic managers commit themselves to help
employees develop and use their skills and talents. The result
is a multitude of personal contributions that create broad corporate success. This is the essence of the new Worth Ethic.

Why can't all managers put the Worth Ethic to work with
immediate success? Very often they haven't experienced the
interpersonal realities of managing. They can think just fine,
but they aren't skilled enough at using their intuition and
emotions to motivate and lead people. They aren't ready to
lead today's skilled, well-paid employees, who are not particularly motivated by needs for security or material possessions,
like employees during the work ethic era. Nor are they motivated by peer pressure, like Japan's work force.

Moreover, they won't learn to lead the new work force in
any short-term training program. Training programs can introduce new information, spark insights, and refine skills. But
they can't change a person for long. If a person can't unleash
others' capabilities to get a job done, that person needs to
change. How is that done? Building on my experience at helping senior managers, I use an eight-step process for change
from the inside out. It empowers managers to get to know
themselves first, and use that insight to change how they work
with people. This CHANGING Process is what makes the
Worth Ethic work.

The Worth Ethic also helps build strong friendships. I
count my co-workers as my friends, and I often find myself
going to them for advice about such concerns as maintaining
my pool or keeping my garage doors functioning. I reciprocate
by sharing my skills and insights on problems with teenagers

and spouses, or suggesting ways to keep their stress levels manageable. But this kind of support and caring is almost expected between friends, whether they are friends from work, from the neighborhood, or wherever. We choose our friends. Actually, it's at work tasks and in the home, where people are together not out of choice but out of economic or biological necessity, that the Worth Ethic's benefits are so striking.

I have always used the Worth Ethic at home, raising my daughter, Catherine. We work together to juggle all our responsibilities. I keep my commitments to her, and she reciprocates with a trustworthiness far beyond her sixteen years. I praise her a lot, both because I know praise works better than punishment and because I am truly proud of her. I know she's proud of me too.

We live on ten acres, high on a ridge, 2,500 feet above Silicon Valley. In good weather, we can see sixty miles south, to Monterey Bay. Out our back door is a five-hundred-acre wildlife reserve. Especially in the spring and summer, when I am more apt to be driving home from work in daylight, I am touched with the beauty of the world around me. At that time of day, on a regular basis, I allow myself to feel gratitude that I'm alive and in this world and especially that I am blessed with work that I love so much. This level of satisfaction and contentment are still rare in the corporate world. I hope *The Worth Ethic* passes this blessing on to you.

I

HEART WORKS
The People-Profit Connection

"To make a living is no longer enough. Work also has to make a life."
—PETER DRUCKER, *Management*

THE COMPANY AS FAMILY

Home is where the heart is. And the heart must come to work, if we are to meet the expectations of the new work force.

More than ever before, people expect to find their worth affirmed at work. Twenty years ago not even 5 percent of our population expected to develop their potential and find satisfaction through work. Today, 40 percent of employees believe they have a fundamental right to self-fulfillment, to develop and use their intellectual and creative abilities to the fullest. They believe they are worth as much to the company as their managers. They want to perform meaningful work that brings value to the world, and they have the latent power to insist on being treated as worthy.

The new work force consists of equal numbers of men and women who were born in the years just after World War II, marry late if ever, live alone for longer periods of their lives, and willingly move far from home, across the continent and across the world, to pursue their work. Singles may constitute the majority of households by the year 2000. They have little or no family support system. They look to work to fill that vacuum and give them a meaningful life that engages their emotions as well as their minds and bodies.

The traditional work force—white, male, married, and sole source of family funds—found worth in its undeniable importance to family, community, and church. Whatever the family, community, and church by default or absence no longer supply, today's new work force expects of its company. The new work force expects to invest its heart at work, and expects a similar commitment from its employer and manager. If managers can somehow meet the expectations of the new work force, they will leverage their human resources to create higher productivity and greater profits.

A PARADIGM SHIFT FOR THE CORPORATION

The obvious, significant implication of these dramatic differences is that the new work force wants and needs to nurture and be nurtured but is far less likely to get the opportunity than the traditional work force. Fewer workers have someone at home to ask for advice and support. Fewer workers have children to work for, plan for, and dream for. Most workers live without the benefit of an extended family nearby. Just as a power vacuum is created when a top manager leaves a company, an emotional vacuum is created when employees live without a social support system in their personal lives.

This is a vacuum the workplace must fill. A transformation is required in America in which the company takes on many roles previously played by the family. Without this major shift, employees' loyalty and productivity will continue to decline.

Five years ago, having trod the traditional path of corporate America, I joined KLA Instruments, a high-technology, high-growth Silicon Valley firm. There I found myself in a company whose culture was founded on reciprocal commitmen' between managers and employees. Certainly I was aware of Hewlett-Packard's leadership in showing respect for the individual. But at KLA I saw employees working longer, harder, and more enthusiastically than in any other place I had worked. As I settled into life in the Valley, I discovered some other corporations that were inspiring their employees to work longer, harder, and with greater involvement, and they weren't all high-tech. What I noticed was that, in these few, special companies, employees' personal needs were being met through work. This was radically different from anything I had observed before.

These companies treated employees as worthy people, deserving of attention, support, and fair rewards. They saw employees as their most vital resource. They built employees' feelings of self-worth, and employees reciprocated by giving their best efforts to create worthy goods and services. The result was a committed work force that loved to work. People do love to work—you probably love it yourself. Most cars, gardens, and bicycles receive considerable elbow grease and knee action on weekends and weekday evenings. As the number of U.S. workers who say they enjoy work more than leisure has declined to 24 percent, these same people go home to rebuild engines, dig in the dirt, cycle for miles, or in myriad ways work hard after "work."

Yet people who work hard at these self-appointed tasks at home waste almost a third of the workday. When they do work, they work at one-fifth of their capabilities. A survey of working Americans was conducted by the Public Agenda Foundation, a nonprofit organization founded in 1975 by Cyrus Vance and Daniel Yankelovich, a significant spokesman for changing U.S. values. This survey reports that fewer than one out of four (23 percent) say they work at full potential, and nearly 50 percent say they do not work any harder than they must to meet basic job requirements. The overwhelming majority (75 percent) say they could significantly increase their performance, and nearly

3

six in ten workers believe people do not work as hard as they used to.

Peter Drucker, a respected observer of management practices, predicts we'll need to boost what we produce by 50 percent over the next ten years yet keep the number of workers stable if we are to remain competitive internationally. This means turning today's average performers into stars and helping star performers surpass all expectations, when most workers don't want to work much at all. At work, anyway.

Why don't we get people to work as hard at work as they do at play? Job satisfaction has declined, says an Opinion Research Corporation of Princeton, N.J. survey, because workers want more "self-expression, self-fulfillment, and personal growth." When the workday ends, they willingly take on tasks that interest, challenge, satisfy, and reward them within their personal value system. They work hard at what they want to do and love to do.

THE WORTH ETHIC

There is no leader without followers. We succeed together or not at all. This is the essential "W.E." of the Worth Ethic, the belief in your indelible self-worth and the fundamental and potential worth of others. The conviction that you are personally capable and have significant contributions to make to the world fosters a belief that others, too, are worthy.

"Work ethic" employees in the early 1900s worked hard at any job they could get because they feared starvation, loved God, or both. The task might have been brain-numbing, their managers cruel, their co-workers exploited, but they worked, anyway. They had to.

Today the majority of us work for far different reasons. We long for proof of our self-worth and a chance to make a difference. Some managers resist the trend toward Worth Ethic values and wish they still had work ethic workers to order

4

around. Worth Ethic managers, on the other hand, acknowledge the legitimate human desire to make a difference as well as the tremendous stake business has in supporting this inner motivation.

In the workplace, managers with a Worth Ethic take a new approach to leading people. They recognize that everyone in the company wants to be capable and powerful. They empower their employees to make significant personal contributions at work by training every person to maximum potential, offering challenges at each level of responsibility, and managing every employee with a flexible organization and caring systems.

Numerous research studies, founded on basic psychological truths, prove that people who receive attention, recognition, and praise from others become more cooperative and harder working. When others give them a measure of control over their work, they become more committed. When others encourage them to grow and develop their potential, they become more loyal to the company and more excited about their future opportunities. None of these advantages can be achieved without the participation of another person, someone willing to share power and praise to create the "W.E." of the Worth Ethic.

Somehow, we managers need to ignite employees' passion for work in the workplace. We can do it, too, if we'll recognize what psychologists in general have known all along: that expedient solutions are just that—handy, useful but selfserving, and that principled solutions require us to invest our attention and our passion at work just as we want employees to do. Like the difference between a one-night stand and a marriage, between being cavalier and committed, between working for a company we move in and out of quickly versus one we expect to stay with for a long time, we need to admit that we do indeed behave differently when we give a damn.

How do we behave when we really care about people, value their contributions to the relationship, and wish them the best of everything they've ever dreamed of or hoped for? We are honest. We are generous. We are committed to supporting their goals.

Hallmark Cards built their business on the phrase, "When you care enough to send the very best." When you care, you don't cheat on a spouse. When you care, you don't cut down a teenager with constant criticism. When you care, you don't hold back your best ideas from a business partner— not unless you choose to deal with a divorce, a runaway child, or a business break-up. When you care about your employees, you are honest with them. You are generous. You are committed. You never manipulate them. And you respect them.

MANAGERS THINK TOO MUCH
AND FEEL TOO SELDOM

This idea of caring about employees comes dangerously close to the idea that we managers should view employees as people as well as resources. It hits the quick of what we have been taught not to do—get involved with employees and empathize with their feelings. We don't listen to their complaints or dreams, unless we're forced to. So what if workers squabble or get bored or feel imprisoned on the job? We can't be bothered by minor complaints, and when they become major labor issues they're beyond our scope.

I don't recommend we stop thinking entirely and try to feel our way caringly through the next complicated project we undertake. I don't recommend we turn meetings into bull sessions about emotions to the exclusion of committing to positive action. I do say this: If we learn the intuitive and interpersonal skills necessary to get in touch with our employees' emotional needs, we will build their self-worth and empower them to drive toward outstanding results and to work like star performers.

We need to be leaders of people, not just managers of projects. The hard-nosed, extract-everything-you-can-from-employees approach to project management is counterproductive. We've learned an expensive lesson as we've watched the Japanese overtake us in productivity. Exquisite number-crunching and analytical controls don't create excellence nor do they motivate employees to produce extraordinary results. The passion goes out of performance when the expectation that people should be self-controlled and rational at work is interpreted by workers as a requirement to leave their hearts at home.

To create highly motivated performers from average employees, we must treat our employees as people—talk with them, listen to their work ideas, and get them involved in projects early on. Unless we do so, we remain ineffective proposers rather than productive implementors of solutions. When our employees don't know what's going on, they certainly can't buy into a solution and implement it enthusiastically. When we include our employees in the process of devising workable solutions to problems, we meet their needs to take part, make a contribution, and feel valuable. Because we listen to their concerns, consider the validity of their objections, and weigh and integrate their ideas as much as is practical, our employees come to trust our good judgment.

Moreover, we come to know their views sufficiently so that, when the time comes to choose between alternate ways of doing things, we already know which solution is going to be backed most enthusiastically. We create a bond of reciprocal trust when we work empathically with our employees, and that trust releases the motivation, energy, and commitment of our employees.

At present, we managers habitually spend more time at work thinking than responding to our own feelings, nagging worries, uneasiness, or other internal experiences, let alone being concerned about whether employees are happy. From 1981 to 1987, two business psychologists, Dick Strayer and Richard Hagberg, working independently, administered two different batteries of psychological tests to over 500 executives. They found that fully 75 percent of them functioned predominantly with their thinking sides rather than with their intuitive, feeling sides. Because these executives lead companies, and are consequently powerful role models for the managers they hire, the people that work for them get the inevitable message that they, too, should spend more time thinking than feeling.

Other research findings bear this out. Fernando Bartolome, visiting professor at Harvard Business School, interviewed forty mid-career male managers and their wives and found that these men saw work as a hyper-masculine world calling for strength, self-reliance, and "a stiff upper lip." They were uncomfortable responding to, and felt no need to deal with, what they saw as the "feminine" world of emotions. They were afraid to abandon their total self-reliance and control. They hesitated to give way to passion and begin to care about their employees.

The need for greater empathy among managers is well documented: Managers with expressive skills perform better and are more successful. In a test at Newark College of Engineering, eleven of twelve company presidents who doubled sales over four years scored abnormally high on intuition. Getting in touch with their gut instincts paid off on the bottom line.

A study by Morgan McCall at the Center for Creative Leadership in Greensboro, North Carolina, disclosed that fast trackers who "derailed" failed primarily because they lacked one of several critical interpersonal skills. Purdue University records indicate that social skills account for fully 85 percent of their engineering graduates' success in business. Thus, we need to develop our feeling sides in order to manage the new work force.

THE NEW WORK FORCE

In *The Affluent Society*, John Kenneth Galbraith labeled the New Class—the educated, salaried professionals most managers are trying to manage today, often without much success. Typically, this new class is somewhere between the ages of 24 and 42 and spent their formative years in the 1960s and 1970s. Half of the work force is female. Foreign-born students come to study and remain to work in professional jobs. Among married couples, the single paycheck family is disappearing. Among women in their early thirties who have not married, 34 percent will never marry. Twenty-five percent of all American adults live alone, a percentage that will climb to between 35 and 50 percent by the year 2000. With these altered demographics have come different personal needs that cannot be met by the traditional work ethic of the industrial age.

The achievement- and peer-oriented adults of the 1950s raised their children in a new way, opening the door to the "New Age" of the 1960s. As a result people are coming to the workplace with new expectations. They're expecting work to include personal satisfaction, a chance to be their best selves, and an opportunity to make a contribution.

Today's employee is likely to come from a new—and increasingly influential—group that the Values and Lifestyles Program, an ongoing ten-year study by Stanford Research Institute (SRI) in Menlo Park, California, dubbed the "inner drivens." They generally start life as the offspring of achievement-oriented families and as such taste the rewards of achievement early on, thanks to their parents. A peculiar thing happens to these "inner drivens": they follow a totally new hierarchy of motivations that focus on feelings such as caring, harmony, loyalty, and personal power. Paychecks are not enough for them — they want psychic rewards as well. Their new social and business ethic is characterized, SRI concludes, by self-determination, concern for the quality of life, decentralization, and more personal control.

These young professionals and specialists aren't the only ones unmotivated by the work ethic of the Industrial Age. As women entered the work force in droves, they tended to bring relationship-oriented values and nurturing skills with them.

They experimented with donning men's suits and adopting their number-and-dollar-oriented work ethic, and we expected them to move steadily into top management positions. After all, their ranks doubled between 1975 and 1985, to 49 million. Yet today they fill no more than 10 percent of all managerial positions and hold only one percent of senior executive positions. They top out in their careers and leave in frustration to start consultancies and entrepreneurial companies.

This is unfortunate because women's soft skills are particularly useful in motivating and integrating innovation. New technology does not convert to marketplace innovation until it is incorporated into products that change the world around us. This critical step requires the motivation, communication, and community-building skills that most women have refined from early childhood. Growing up female often means being well supported in exploring the intuitive and emotional side of life. Girls are encouraged from a very early age to get in touch with and articulate their emotional experiences and, as a result, many find it easy to empathize with others.

Although in most corporate cultures women still believe they have to suppress their emotions to progress in their careers and to be respected by male managers, the balance is shifting slightly. A few leading-edge corporations are beginning to recognize their need for employees who can facilitate communications and achieve the employee commitment they're after. This is just the sort of thing many women have traditionally been good at.

A PARADIGM SHIFT FOR MANAGERS

Twenty years ago, a top executive at a systems analysis company bragged to me, "We're coining money with our new contracts and we don't have a dime in equipment or other tangible assets. Our assets are our people. They come in that door every day and when I don't need them, I let them go."

Mean? No. Simply uncaring. He was just another hard-nosed businessman paid only to think and act. Never mind the heart.

Today hard-nosed solutions don't work. Why not? Robert Reich, in *Tales of a New America*, calls for a revitalization of industry by encouraging people to "... pool their efforts, insights, and enthusiasm without fear of exploitation." Reich touches on the fundamental reason employees fail to contribute their full capabilities consistently. They feel exploited. And, honestly, so do we. Like them, we hold back. More than 30 percent of the 1,200 middle managers surveyed by the New York–based National Institute of Business Management said they would be happier working for other companies. We managers bring our bodies to work. We put our minds to the present task. But, like our employees, we don't engage our whole selves in our work either.

It's time we did. We can affirm our employees' worth. What's required of us is a paradigm shift that allows each of us, managers and employees alike, to move from an adversarial to a collaborative position. Managers must go from exploiting employees as a limited and disposable resource to supporting, developing, and valuing them as a potentially limitless resource.

Such an exemplary shift demands a totally different view of the managerial role. You abandon your task-management role and take responsibility for using your employees' and your own capabilities to the fullest. You admit to a connectedness in which they are a part of your support system and you are a part of theirs. You work hard and well together, with the involvement and satisfaction you once got from working on your car or in your garden. You put your heart in your work and, as a result, make it easy for your employees to do the same.

I'm not proposing something entirely new. We've all experienced the enthusiasm and passion of loving what we're doing. Think back to when you were a teenager: You completed your homework assignments, but I'll bet you dedicated yourself to the marching band, the football team, the debate club, or the swim team.

Most of us, from the time we first learned sufficient social skills to play together, invested tremendous energy in trying to outrun and outscore our opponents. We played at soldiering as children, scuttling between bushes and hiding behind trees to trap the "enemy." We crouched way down under things and climbed high out of sight to escape capture and keep a step ahead of the enemy. We invested our efforts in activities that stirred our imagination and enthusiasm. We committed ourselves to a cause bigger than ourselves. We did so because we sought to belong and we wanted to be necessary.

The need still beckons. We need to belong and to be needed not just as young people in the first third of life, not simply by our family and friends as we grow up, not just on weekends as adults, but all day, every day, all through our lives. We need to feel that we're necessary and that our contributions are appreciated at work. When our worth is acknowledged, we experience a profound change in our health and the ultimate productivity of our minds and bodies.

At a very fundamental level it's been shown that all humans, managers included, are healthier when they feel the results of caring. Harvard psychologists David McClelland and Carol Kirshnit measured subjects' levels of IG-A, a chemical in the body that increases immunity to colds and viruses, after they watched several films. They found the levels remained unchanged in the participants, except after they watched a film about Mother Teresa and her work among the poor. Double-checking results, the psychologists asked viewers to recall past times when they had caring experiences, and again their IG-A levels rose, this time for an hour or more. These results came from merely observing or thinking about caring behaviors. Imagine what happens when people have their worth affirmed directly!

Psychologist Karl W. Kuhnert found in a survey of over 200 manufacturing employees that when people perceive a high validity to their work, they feel more secure about their jobs. This makes sense. But more than this, Kuhnert also found that feelings of job security predicted employees' well-being more than any other factor. The more secure people felt in their jobs, the more they believed their work was important and the healthier they were physically and mentally. We don't just want to do something important—we actually need to do something important to maintain our well-being. That "we" includes us managers.

Sure, we'd like to commit ourselves to something grand and glorious. We hunger for the big win. But what do we get? An occasional "Atta boy." We're not part of the inside team. We rarely feel connected to the company in any significant way. What we've come to expect from the company, all too often, is merely a paycheck. It's as if at the bottom of every ad for managers and employees these words appeared: "Hearts need not apply." Does the company know we exist as real human beings? We're expected to work without significant promotions or pay increases, and certainly without many psychic rewards, dedicated only to getting the job done wherever we are and whoever pays us.

We managers, too, need and want to have our worth affirmed. So deep down, we already know a lot about motivating the new work force to greater efforts because we know what motivates us. Then why don't we do something about it?

A PROGRAM FOR CHANGING TO THE WORTH ETHIC

As a manager, you are a complex person handling a complex role. Substantive change is difficult because, however unpleasant or awkward your present way of doing things, the results of your actions are at least predictable. Wait until the last moment to write a complicated project proposal, then dump the massive typing job on your overworked secretary. You'll feel apologetic or guilty for a while. But after that, everything will go on as usual. When you try to change your behavior, you're not only uncertain what new behavior to substitute, you're not sure what the consequences will be.

Sometime in the past, you've undoubtedly tried to change

your management style without shifting your internal point of view. Think of all those good ideas you picked up in management training, ideas you had every intention of installing back in your department but never did. You didn't really drop the idea for lack of time or support, although those may have been your excuses. What actually happened was that you tried to superimpose new behaviors on top of old attitudes—and it didn't work.

For this reason, I'll help you explore your internal points of view. Where do you begin? The Worth Ethic shows up in your personal integrity, in the ways you use your personal power, and in your willingness to find deeper meaning in your work, to use your intuition, to develop your talents, to approve of yourself, to reward yourself for work well done, and to manage stress and live a balanced life. In areas you are dissatisfied with yourself and your relationship to the new work force, you'll learn how to change your outdated attitudes through a process of change from the inside out, a process very like the one I use to coach executives in my consulting practice. These are the eight steps of the CHANGING Process:

C   *Create a concrete description of the desired change.*
H   *Honestly examine your motivation to change.*
A   *Abandon the old behavior in your imagination.*
N   *Name the change positively.*
G   *Give attention to payoffs.*
I   *Imagine the past and see how you behaved.*
N   *Nail down the new behavior using mental rehearsal.*
G   *Graduate to the new behavior.*

As you experience these steps, you'll learn how to stretch your emotional muscles. Feeling is a lot like playing racquetball. Thinking about it won't increase your skill much. You have to practice and you need to know your own feelings as well as you know your own mind.

If you're curious to know what it's like to get in touch with your emotions, try asking yourself, "What am I feeling right now?" Then set your digital watch to ring in half an hour. When it does, check inside yourself and see what's going on. You may draw a blank at first, but persist. After a few days of paying attention to your own inner experiences, you'll begin to detect subtle gut instincts that will guide you in your decision making and strengthen your leadership.

You face three levels of change:

PHASE ONE: For a smooth, successful change, your beliefs, values, and attitudes need to shift. You need to get to know yourself better and come to like yourself a lot. Begin by treating yourself as a member of the family. Family members don't take advantage of one another. They don't exploit one another. They give one another the attention they need—they give a damn. You can't care about someone else until you first care about yourself.

The process of changing from the inside out is like creating a candle by dipping it repeatedly in hot wax. You begin with a wick, then add layer upon layer of candle wax. In the end, the wick is barely visible, yet without it the candle would quickly go out. With it, the candle sheds light. Similarly, by internalizing the Worth Ethic you empower yourself to change your work habits and management style permanently.

PHASE TWO: Once you have claimed the Worth Ethic as yours, you will use its qualities to relate more empathetically, and therefore more effectively, with co-workers and employees. You will change your management style to bring it into alignment with the Worth Ethic values. You will show outwardly that you care about the people with whom you work. While some managers may not share your values, they will find your results persuasive. Groups managed with Worth Ethic values consistently outperform groups led by functionally competent managers who are without compassion.

In *Thriving on Chaos*, Tom Peters reminds us of the power of this kind of example: " . . . the manager's minute-to-minute actions provide a living model of his or her strategic vision. Modeling, behavioral scientists tell us with rare accord, is the chief way people learn."

PHASE THREE: You will make the change to the Worth Ethic environment a real possibility throughout your entire company because people will observe your new management practices. People don't change their attitudes easily. By contrast, observed practices are a powerful agent for change.

The Worth Ethic management style and practices empower you to lead the new work force. Peter Drucker writes, in *Management*, "Leadership is the raising of a man's performance to higher standards, the building of a man's personal understanding beyond its normal limitations. Nothing better prepares the ground for such leadership than a spirit of management that confirms in the day-to-day practices the organization's strict principles of conduct and responsibility, high standards of performance, and respect for the individual and his work." The Worth Ethic is your statement of principles, but more than that, it becomes your statement of beliefs.

Can you expect that a change which, for you, began on the inside and worked its way out, will work in the reverse direction for those around you? No, you can't. At some point, the people around you must begin their own three-tiered change from the inside out. Change is almost never a simple matter of attending a training session or watching a demonstration, then putting it into effect when you get back to your office.

You have probably come back from training programs revved up and ready to put new ideas into action, then found your energy begin to wane after a week or two. It's a universal experience. We tell ourselves we failed because we didn't receive enough support from our organization, or we didn't have the time. But what really happens is that the good ideas get layered on top of old attitudes and beliefs, and there isn't enough internal momentum to create real change. Your employees and co-workers, too, must change from the inside out. Once you change your own attitudes and beliefs and make the Worth Ethic visible, you will inspire them to change along with you. If you provide the leadership, they will follow in your footsteps.

THE MAJOR ROADBLOCK TO THE WORTH ETHIC

In the United States, most of us have been told that it is unnecessary and even a little strange to get close to people outside our immediate family. We're expected to maintain distance, not create connectedness. As we progress from home to school to work, parents, teachers, and managers insist that we learn to control ourselves. We shouldn't cry, shout, or gloat in public. They show few emotions themselves.

As children, we were probably cuddled and soothed when we cried. But in adolescence, we probably didn't see our dad express his feelings toward us. As mature adults, we're aware of intense emotions such as anger or sadness. But we've taught ourselves to ignore and suppress all but the strongest emotions until we're safely at home. Perhaps even there, all alone, we deny our emotions and convert them to ulcers, high blood pressure, or other subtle symptoms of stress.

This isn't the way it has to be. Many attribute their success to the ability to relate easily and warmly to people. They make sure the people around them feel valued and important, challenged to perform and explore new arenas, and that they will be rewarded by plenty of recognition and support. We're currently bombarded with stories by captains of industry who are willing to share their dreams, passions, strategies, and feelings with us. Lee Iacocca has become an authentic folk hero; Armand Hammer, Ted Turner, Frank Borman, John Sculley have all revealed their embarrassments and foibles, joys and successes.

I imagine you've had such a leader in your past, someone who inspired you to do your absolute personal best. In my senior year in college, I signed up for a required freshman-level psychology course. It was taught by a teaching assistant, a motivated, enthusiastic doctoral student who held after-hour discussion groups. He encouraged me to test my beliefs about myself and to examine my life for mountain peak and pit experiences. Out of our association, I came to respect my own skill at working with people, leading them, and helping them to help themselves. My fascination with psychology was born, and I switched from engineering to psychology in graduate school. No doubt you, too, have known a person who made you feel a little prouder, stand a little taller, and work a little harder, who enabled you to produce something out of the ordinary. That person made you feel warm and comfortable as well as exhilarated and challenged.

If you were lucky, it's how you were raised by your parents. For good or ill, we're all very much the product of our parental programming. How we are raised dictates how we value and use our talents, the goals we set for ourselves, the hangups we carry around with us, the expectations that prompt our adult experiences, and how we interpret what goes on around us. You became yourself by imitating and identifying with those around you when you were young. Those early experiences defined your self-image and created your perception of the world. Today they determine to a great extent what, as an adult, turns you on and makes you run.

Typically, the method of raising children reflects the reality of the world as parents perceive it. These influential adults teach us what they think we need to know to get along. In the 1920s to 1940s, children were expected to be little adults. Our own parents were expected to respect their elders and to speak when spoken to. They were probably punished if they did not obey promptly. Their parents trained them to conform and made few concessions to their immaturity because they knew that, when our parents went out into the world, they'd be treated unsympathetically and maybe even rudely.

Our own parents probably didn't like being treated that way, and as a group they took a somewhat different attitude in raising us. They saw themselves less as trainers, whip in hand, and more as teachers ready to encourage us. Consequently, we were raised in a kindly autocracy. We felt our parents were at least willing to help us learn what we needed to be taught. If you are a parent today, you've probably moved even further away from coercion, toward supportive parenting. Over the past twenty-five years parents have tried to be coaches to their children, giving stimulation and guidance rather than direction and control.

What I'm saying is that you feel comfortable in a thinking environment because of how you were raised. For the same reason, your children, your younger employees, in fact almost all members of the new work force, feel more comfortable in an environment that's open, collaborative, and caring. Peter Drucker writes: "The knowledge worker is not productive under the spur of fear, only self-motivation and self-direction can make him productive. He has to be achieving in order to produce at all." The work force has changed. Often the nature of its tasks have changed as well, and as a result, productivity is not only hard to inspire, it's even hard to define in the case of engineers, teachers, scientists, and other knowledge workers. To lead this new work force, you'd better understand it and empathize with it.

Since you spend nearly half of your waking hours at work, to deny yourself personal involvement with the people there is like trying to run with only one leg. You are using only half of your resources—your thinking side—when you could be using the other half, your feeling side, as well. You can make the difference in your employees' productivity and your organization's profitability. You can get connected to the people who work with you. You and your employees can let loose and love working at work just as much as you love "working" at your health club, on the golf course, or in your garden.

Ultimately, when enough individuals are committed to this long-range strategy and when enough external changes are made in the systems, procedures, and structures that help your organization operate, your company will begin to reflect Worth Ethic values. Your company will be nudged persistently toward effectively supporting and working with the new work force and its Worth Ethic. The Worth Ethic promises a high level of employee job satisfaction and productivity with its emphasis on "W.E." rather than "I," so that in the end, your employees' personal successes will create broad success for you and your company.

2

CIRCLE OF TRUST
What Goes Around, Comes Around

"There is no such thing as a minor lapse of integrity."
—TOM PETERS, *Thriving on Chaos*

In my first job, I was a survey analyst in Saigon, during the military pullout. My college classmates had marched for peace and protested the Vietnam War at sit-ins, but I chose to see if I could promote peace by working within the system. My job was to measure the impact of a land redistribution program that had been designed to "win the hearts and minds of Vietnamese peasants." But the data didn't come out that way.

When I reported these negative findings to my supervisor, he told me to reanalyze the data and draw the anticipated conclusions. I objected. But caught between doing the right thing and keeping my job, I settled for keeping my name off the report. I felt sullied and distrustful, I lost pride in a job well done, and my productivity as an analyst declined dramatically. Extrapolate my experience along with that of every worker asked to fudge a figure or look the other way, and you get a glimpse of the enormous loss of productivity prompted by managers when they foster or simply tolerate unethical practices.

The paradigm shift to the Worth Ethic requires meticulous standards of integrity. We affirm our own and our employees' worth when we manage with unimpeachable integrity. Moreover, our integrity earns employees' trust and, as a consequence, permits them to invest their hearts at work. The company that stands by its product and requires honorable dealings with its suppliers, customers, and employees can expect to be rewarded with hard working, loyal employees. The circle of trust is created.

Unfortunately, as Robert Allen reports in *Organizational Dynamics,* more than 90 percent of managers believe that organizations tend to encourage unethical, dishonest, and inhumane behavior. Believing that an organization is unethical, managers find it easy to sidestep moral responsibility. Employees can similarly excuse their own expedient actions. In other words, when we managers lack integrity, we cause employees' deep and very counterproductive belief in "rot at the top," a profound distrust of business or government and often both together.

Once we reinforce an ingrained distrust of organizational ethics with a perceived lack of personal integrity within managers, we create employees who are ashamed of their companies and the products they produce. They don't feel good about the work they're doing. The work's not worthy, so they can't put their hearts in it. And as a consequence, they don't work hard.

WHO LACKS INTEGRITY?

In the old work ethic, we took integrity for granted. We were shocked by obvious breaches of integrity, such as the Wall Street insider-trading scandal in 1986 and 1987. But we reassured ourselves: We personally never engaged in blatant breaches of ethics—such headline affairs were far removed

from our daily lives. We could not precipitate major consequences by our minor lapses in integrity. Right?

Wrong. We can claim sterling ethical standards, but if we
fail to live up to them, if we act without honor, we cause
problems. Suppose you're a Quality Assurance manager who'll
create havoc if you buck the system, so you overlook a few
quality discrepancies. Or a project manager who won't look
like a superhero if you admit you've got a problem, so you
cover it up. Or a general manager with a tight budget, and you
go along with company policy and sell the customer on paying
for upgrades that were part of the original contract specs. Or a
sales manager routinely cheating ever so slightly on expense
accounts, a product development manager purposely under-
estimating the difficulty of developing a product dear to your
heart, or any manager opting for the expedient instead of the
right way in the rush of a day's business.

What are you? If you're like one of these managers, you're
typical of the late 1980s, trying to hold on to a job in a business
environment that rewards short-term approaches to making
money and making more money. If you're like one of these
managers, you're operating without complete integrity and
you're part of the reason U.S. business has lost its competitive
edge.

Without belief in a company's ethical fiber and a sense of
pride in the products they help make, employees are inclined
to take the company for all they can. They socialize, make
personal phone calls, arrive late to work and leave early. They
take sick leave when they aren't sick. They delay working on
projects until a deadline looms, then work in a rush with little
regard for quality but plenty of pleasure in any overtime that's
"required." Treated by anonymous manufacturing methods as
if they, too, were machines, feeling exploited and manipulated, they don't care about their employer.

THE COST OF LOW ETHICAL STANDARDS IS HIGH

Faced with this tremendous loss of employee productivity, why would companies even consider scuttling ethical standards? Having acknowledged the value of working hard and well with employees, why would managers ever condone dishonesty within their organizations? A common justification is the basic need for profitability, a justification unfounded in fact.

Good ethics and good business go hand in hand. In 1983, James Burke, chairman of Johnson & Johnson, commissioned a study to compare the profitability of *Fortune* 500 companies with twenty-five companies with a long history of serving the public. The study showed the profit growth rate of the public-service companies exceeded that of the *Fortune* 500 companies by 69 percent. When Barbara Spencer, management professor at Clemson University, and Richard Wokutchem, professor at Virginia Polytechnic Institute, compared 130 manufacturing companies based on the size of their charitable contributions, their history of illegal activities, and their earnings, the "sinning" companies performed considerably worse than the ordinary to "saintly" groups.

According to Kenneth Blanchard, reporting in *Executive Excellence,* 1987, the Ethics Research Center in Washington found that $30,000 invested in a composite of the Dow Jones companies thirty years ago would be worth 12 percent of the value of the same $30,000 invested among twenty-one companies with a written code of principles, for whom "serving the public was central to their being."

Johnson & Johnson took its Tylenol product off the shelves immediately after the tampering incident and retained its strong market position. Beech-Nut Nutrition Corporation, which manufactures baby foods, lied about its phony apple juice and found the cover-up costly. In 1981, Beech-Nut's director of research suspected that a supplier was selling the company fake apple concentrate. Management refused to listen to him. Ten months later, the company ignored the findings of a trade group's private investigator. Had Beech-Nut acted on either of these warnings, the company could have admitted to a civil violation of food and drug laws, paid a fine, dumped its $3.5 million dollar juice inventory, and attracted some bad publicity. It would have endured a small squall, in contrast to the major hurricane to come. But instead of facing up to its ethical problem, the company continued to sell the tainted juice, riled government investigators, and eventually pled guilty to 215 felony counts. Beech-Nut lost sales, credibility, and legal fees—perhaps as much as $25 million in all. Seven years later, it was still getting bad press from the failed cover-up. The state of New York announced in May of 1988 that Beech-Nut paid a $250,000 state fine just to settle the state's charges against it.

Shady ethics are costly. Some costs may seem small on an individual basis, but they add up quickly. Consider the snowballing costs of the minor thefts of pens and paper, having lunch on the company expense account, or doing personal errands on company time. And consider the cost of sick leave when employees call in sick but really aren't.

Other costs are more obvious. Studies by Robert Nathan, Irwin Ross and Marshall Clinard show that dishonesty causes 30 percent of all business failures, fraud and abuse waste 10 percent of government budgets, and white-collar crime costs ten times more than street crime. Herchell Britton, executive vice president of the Burns International Security Service, says that in a year white-collar crime adds up to more than $70 billion. Every day retailers lose goods worth $20 million, more of it from employee theft than from shoplifting. Robert Half International surveyed 330 large- and medium-sized companies about time-theft—that is, the deliberate and persistent waste of paid time—through getting to work late, leaving early, and doing everything but work while there. The survey concludes that time-theft costs American business $170 billion annually.

These figures represent not simply failures of integrity by

individuals in business, but the failure of businesses to build environments that encourage honesty. What happens when employees see secretaries do personal work for their managers or observe executives getting by with expense account thefts? They often join in the action. A woman manager from an East Coast company told me her manager tacked huge laundry expenses on to his monthly report. At a company party, she heard the president wonder bemusedly if her manager had bought the Chinese laundry yet. That settled her own doubts. When her second garment bag of that year gave out on a business trip, she blithely charged a new, higher quality bag to her own expense account.

BLOCKS TO INTEGRITY

The reason companies operate unethically is that top management sets the tone and creates policy, but the individual manager interprets policy and takes action or not. That individual manager probably believes fervently in his or her own personal integrity. A 1986 Korn/Ferry study asked 4,500 senior executives, the people who build and maintain companies, to rate what contributed most to their success. Integrity was named by 71 percent of the respondents and stood at the top of the composite list. The high rating of integrity is a sign that we've made a shift toward the Worth Ethic in principle. But in practice, our behavior still reflects old standards left over from the traditional work ethic.

What blocks our integrity in business? The problem is ambiguity, the fact that an action can seem to be either right or wrong, depending on our point of view. To accomplish the shift toward the Worth Ethic paradigm, it's time to begin the first level of change, the shift in our beliefs, attitudes, and values relative to ethics and integrity.

YOU ACT OUT OF EXPEDIENCY

Suppose you're a manager at a successful start-up company with enormous cash flow and production problems. The company needs solutions quickly and the management team demands action from you at any cost. Just what does "at any cost" really mean? Does it include releasing a product before it meets specifications, then using the first few customers to test and improve the product? Clearly this would have some consequences in terms of customer relations, unless the customer has agreed to be a test site. It also would communicate to the work force, which would be aware of claims made in the company's new-product releases, that it's all right to mislead customers. Does it also mean that the company might renege on commitments to its employees, too? They suspect the answer is yes. So how far backward can you bend, getting product out the door, before your employees begin to question your integrity?

Or suppose you're a manager at a mature company that is up against it to keep market share, and you've been told to cut back on costs somehow. Does "somehow" include going along with top management's recommendation to transfer the older, more highly paid employees to a contract shortly before completion, so you can lay off these high overhead people? How long can you display shaky integrity before your employees get the message your integrity is for sale?

We managers may yearn to be free of contradictions, unworthy motives, and disquieted consciences. We may wish we were like Sir Galahad, with the strength of ten because our hearts are pure. But we act, all too frequently, out of expediency. We should be more concerned about building trust.

YOU DON'T QUITE TRUST THE COMPANY

Doing things the honorable way sometimes takes longer, costs more, or is more trouble. That's why we choose the short-term, expedient way instead. We don't quite trust our company or top management to stand by us when our deadlines and budget get stretched and the customer gets antsy. Or outraged. Expedient actions seem to grease the wheels of business. And that may be true, in the short-term.

However, over the long run, expedient actions lead employees to view management with distrust and suspicion. Distrustful, they are likely to think that any attempts we make to build trust are a ruse. Distrustful, they hoard the bad news, so underlying problems go unnoticed. Distrustful, they devise inappropriate solutions to problems in an attempt to avoid confrontation. Joint problem-solving efforts are nearly impossible without mutual trust.

If you have ever run into trouble on a project because one of your employees didn't tell you that you had a problem until too late, then you know exactly how much trouble lack of trust can cause. Suspicion makes people poor performers. In *The Leadership Challenge,* Jim Kouzes and Barry Posner describe a study conducted for the branches of the Life Insurance Agency Management Association that concluded that the main difference between low-performance groups and high-performance groups was the degree to which employees said they trusted their immediate supervisors.

A team that trusts its leader and its members makes better decisions. A research study by D. E. Zand, summarized in Kouzes and Posner's book, showed that a group of business executives who were told to expect trusting behavior had far better results in reaching a difficult decision than the group that expected untrusting behavior. The trusting group were also more satisfied with the meeting, more motivated to implement the decision, and felt higher levels of collaboration and team spirit. No wonder, then, that they outperformed the untrusting group.

If trust is so essential, how do the company, top management, and you as an individual get the trust you need? You have to earn it. At KLA, we saw trust begin to build at an offsite training program. First, we climbed up a four-foot ladder and fell backward into the hands of the people we worked with. We learned someone was there to catch us if we fell. Then we tackled a twenty-foot wall together. We learned to trust first a little and then a lot.

YOU ARE INCONSISTENT

There's no such thing as being a little bit pregnant, slightly unethical, or somewhat unwilling to trust someone else. In each case, you either are or you are not.

I know a talented business consultant whose life's work is helping people. Once, when a large company overpaid him by $1,000, he kept the money. Now, I don't believe that was right. But he did. His thinking went like this: I am short of cash to develop new training programs; I know that the huge company won't miss the money; I am prepared to return it if asked, but I believe this error gives me needed money to develop a new program that will benefit a lot of people. If the corporation had known about the thousand dollars, could it have derived a better benefit for those same employees? We'll never know.

Would the consultant approve of a firm that kept his money, if by mistake he overpaid a bill? Probably not. He and others like him determine right by the time, place, pressures, and contingencies of the moment. They deny any constant right or wrong such as the Golden Rule of "Do unto others . . ." or Gandhi's prohibition against "commerce without morality." They decide to take action not on principle but on expedience. That is, the usual question they pose is, "Will it work?" Not, "Is it right?"

Contrast this ethical standard with Cherryll Sevy-Tam, a KLA consultant who was once overpaid by $500. Cherryll called me at once to find out how to return the money. My own respect for her jumped immediately because I knew, and I am sure she also knew, that Accounts Payable is so remote from the actual work groups of our company that we would never have known this error had occurred if she hadn't called about it.

I believe this sort of behavior brings its own return. Because Cherryll treats her business customers with honesty, she provokes ethical behavior toward herself in business. For example, I could never cancel a "handshake" agreement with Cherryll or dispute her billings. At KLA, we like Cherryll, and we use her skills whenever we can.

You, like Cherryll, can earn the respect of others by holding yourself accountable for what you do. You can install the Worth Ethic and raise the ethical standards where you work by interrupting any cycle of unethical behavior that exists there. You can confront the moral code in your own life and resolve to act with honor in the future. In this way you convey two very important messages to your employees: that you expect them to act honorably toward both the customer and the company, and that they can expect to be treated honorably by you and your organization.

PHASE ONE: CHANGE WITHIN

An essential jumping-off place for change is to recognize and admit the truth about ourselves. Right now, notice your own feelings about acting with integrity. I expect that you're "for" integrity in business dealings rather than "against" it. But how essential is it to you, really? What's your true belief, deep down?

In general, I developed the CHANGING Process to help you sort back through your life and recall why your feeling side is less completely developed than your thinking side. This process is repeated throughout the book for each major area in which the Worth Ethic is played out. It will lay the foundation for developing your intuitive and interpersonal skills so that you can get in touch with the new work force and its Worth Ethic. To help the change process along in each area I'll share either a personal change or the actual experience of an executive I've coached to a successful shift in attitude and behavior. I have disguised the identities but not the life experiences in the hope that these open discussions will lead you to examine your own life with clarity and courage.

Right now, take a look at how you do business. Examine the borderline areas where you know your integrity comes up short. Maybe your integrity is tainted but others don't seem to either notice or care. For example, do you ever make a promise you know you can't keep? If you don't like what you see, choose a more ethical way of working.

The CHANGING Process will help you change your point of view if you let it. I hope you will take advantage of this opportunity to become aware of your feelings and get to know yourself better. Most of all, I hope you become more caring toward yourself. All the rest follows from that one change.

C   CREATE A CONCRETE DESCRIPTION
OF THE DESIRED CHANGE.

Being as brutally honest as possible, specifically describe your lapses in integrity.

Bob Carroll was sharp, creative, and ambitious. I was asked to work with Bob in an Individual Development Program for six months while the company's top management team considered moving him from manager of the marketing department within a product division to general manager of the entire division.

The promotion seemed a bit of a stretch but well-deserved. Then the company vice president confided that he had one major concern: Could Bob command the respect and support of his peers? If Bob's promotion caused too much turnover, it wasn't a viable decision. The assessment phase of the program gave me an opportunity to ask Bob if he thought he could handle a big promotion. He said, "Sure, I captained the soccer team in high school. I was president of my fraternity at State. I've been competitive all my life and I got a lot of good visibility for my marketing strategies and a project I headed up last year. I suppose I've spent my whole life working toward that kind of opportunity."

Bob's open smile was the kind you expect to find on a nine-year-old kid. I was frankly surprised when, during interviews with his manager and the two other department managers at Bob's level, I heard these people use the words "guerrilla tactics" and "manipulative" and "devious" to describe his business style. One said he thought Bob's unwillingness to share credit for what he'd accomplished showed a "genuine lack of integrity." Then I sent out a questionnaire to twenty people Bob said he had worked closely with in the company. The survey results showed a man who'd certainly never stolen a pencil or misused his secretary's time, yet his whole pattern indicated some shoddiness in the area of integrity. A department manager observed that Bob frequently estimated the volume potential for new products off the top of his head, for example. He seemed to be more interested in impressing his boss and the president than in ensuring that his group delivered excellent results as a team. Bob didn't show up as a likely future leader, worthy of respect by his peers.

Bob and I discussed the assessment results for several hours on a Friday afternoon. I wanted him to have the weekend to think over what the assessment was telling him. Bob believed strongly in his own ethics and at first defended his actions vigorously. He agreed that he "worked the system," that he worked behind the scenes to sell his ideas and wasn't always open with his manager and his peers about the opposition he encountered. But he refused to see this behavior as devious. He also agreed he was manipulative, but he saw this as an essential component of his ability to influence others. Still, he couldn't deny what the survey was telling him: The people he worked with felt he got his victories at their expense.

H HONESTLY EXAMINE YOUR MOTIVATION TO CHANGE.

Is this one of those changes someone else is trying to foist off on you, or are you genuinely motivated to change yourself?

Bob believed that his past success had come because people saw him as someone who got things done. He hadn't failed to see that other people contributed to his success. But to his way of thinking, taking credit for what his group did and using guerrilla tactics were just expected behavior in business. "Why should I change behaviors that have worked so well for me in the past?" he challenged. Bob and I talked about his successes and how he'd achieved them, and he finally admitted, "Maybe, to others, my actions do seem like working the system and hogging the spotlight." When he realized his somewhat "oily" behaviors had created distrust in the people who worked with him, he became more motivated to change. He also realized that the people he worked with day by day must respect him and his ethical standards; otherwise he would never be seen as a true leader. This had the serious consequence of limiting him to the department manager level for life.

A ABANDON THE OLD BEHAVIOR IN YOUR IMAGINATION.

Allow yourself to imagine what your life would be like without this problem behavior. Almost immediately this begins to point you toward change. Confront a tough dilemma in your imagination, such as a situation where the organization wants you to do one thing but you believe a more difficult or costly alternative will be better in the long run. Mentally, act without the old behavior. Be the changed you—in your imagination—with all the concomitant risks, consequences, and victories.

This was a tough step for Bob. He had trouble imagining himself as direct and straightforward. How would he ever accomplish what he wanted if he acted completely aboveboard? Would he lose respect from his work group when they realized how much he depended on their ideas?

In our next meeting, Bob said, "I can imagine myself in staff meetings, sharing credit for a project that was well done, but I see people looking at one another, muttering, 'Where's the old Bob gone to?'" He was sure they'd be leery of his motives. Later Bob said, "I keep hearing myself trying to sell top management on my latest marketing theme, and I keep hearing them say no. If I don't rely on my guerrilla tactics to work the system and convince them that my programs are worthwhile, I'll need to be far more skilled at direct persuasion." He saw that this wasn't going to be easy.

Once Bob recognized his skill deficits, he began to imagine working to improve his relationships with his work group and the heads of other departments. He saw that he'd need to spend more time paying attention to other people's ideas and interests, but he also thought he might like building more rapport with his peers. "I've always sort of envied the lunch bunch, the guys who talk about work problems over lunch," he admitted. He imagined taking more time in meetings, soliciting views, and getting "buy in" from his work group. He imagined spending more time looking at programs from the point of view of top management and other department managers, before he attempted to convert them to his point of view. With clear and concise scenarios of how the programs would benefit the entire company long term, he saw himself successfully convert them to his point of view, in his imagination. And his methods were all direct and up front.

N   NAME THE CHANGE POSITIVELY.

Write out how you want to be with respect to your integrity. This should be one or two short sentences that you can remember easily and say over and over to yourself to get the "feel" of the change you are beginning.

For Bob, the clearest statement was, "I function with the highest integrity." This meant he would be direct and straightforward in dealing with people and selling his ideas. It meant he would look for opportunities to share credit. It meant no more wheedling behind the scenes.

G   GIVE ATTENTION TO PAYOFFS.

Your behavior must have brought you some things you perceived as positive or you would not have incorporated it into your behavior repertoire. So examine these "payoffs." Look closely for the reinforcements that tend to keep the old behavior in place.

Clearly Bob's self-esteem was supported, over the years, by the hero image he'd contrived to create. As the oldest of three boys, he was the biggest and looked like the smartest of the three. In college, he stood out in sports and at the fraternity. "Sure, I depended on other guys to run off the ball for me, in soccer, but that's their job," Bob told me. *He* got the cheers, not them, and that didn't seem to bother him much. He competed successfully with his fraternity brothers for girlfriends, too, gaining social skills and finding more payoffs for using glitz to get what he wanted. Throughout early adulthood, Bob got a lot of accolades and promotions because he looked good, even though it was often at the expense of other people.

I IMAGINE THE PAST AND SEE HOW YOU BEHAVED.

Look carefully at your motivations, but be kind to yourself and nonjudgmental. What you did in the past, you did because it was the best approach available to you at the time. Most of our behavior habits began during early childhood, and at that time they were adaptive and probably necessary. We lay down patterns that later become life themes.

Allow your mind to drift back and forth between the recent past in your work life and the distant past in your childhood, looking carefully at different situations involving ethics and integrity. Pay particular attention to any core events that you generalized into a particular theme. For example, "I'm not as cute as my younger sister; I don't get as much attention," may have gotten shortened to "I don't get enough attention." This attitude may reveal itself in actions that compromise your integrity but let you win.

Bob told me that as an adult he felt embarrassed, uncomfortable, and sad around his younger brothers, neither of whom were as successful as he was. Looking back at their childhood together, he imagined sharing the credit with them more often, like the time when they all pitched in to build a tree house but his parents said they "knew" he'd done most of the work. And that simply wasn't true.

When he thought about it, he saw that he would have come out on top in any backyard game because he was the oldest and biggest. He didn't have to compete so strongly with his brothers. He realized they might have flourished and been somewhat more successful if their own self-esteem hadn't been repeatedly at stake in dinnertime discussions about schoolwork, girlfriends, and athletic skills.

Next he remembered one particular soccer game in which he emerged as the major star. He admitted to himself that, in fact, his team had barely won. Several times in his senior year, if he'd been less eager to hog the glory, the team could have won more easily than they did. He thought they might have been state champions instead of losing in the district playoffs.

Bob thought back to how he'd used people in the past. He seemed to regret, most of all, the loss of a friend he'd made when he first came to the company. The man's name was Joe Walker, he was a department manager, and Bob had liked Joe immediately. Bob said, "We were close for a few months. Then Joe gave me the cold shoulder at an offsite meeting and actually seemed jealous of me. It made me mad, because I hadn't done anything to hurt him. I didn't have to—I knew I was on the fast track, and he wasn't. But I really liked the guy." With my prompting, Bob sat back and imagined he had been more cooperative and helpful to Joe. He imagined being with Joe but not trying to outdo him. He imagined showing Joe how to get in tight with his marketing group so his own projects got good support, and he imagined sharing his ideas with Joe. He saw that Joe would have felt less closed out, might have contributed something good to Bob's ideas, and certainly could have given him useful support early on. Bob admitted he'd honestly never thought he could get satisfaction from helping someone else rather than beating him.

**N   NAIL DOWN THE NEW BEHAVIOR
USING MENTAL REHEARSAL.**

Look forward to work situations that you'll soon face. Imagine setbacks occurring, imagine facing ethical dilemmas, imagine situations in which you used to compromise your integrity because you felt the company was forcing you to make decisions you didn't, at heart, feel good about. Practice on five or six different situations to build your ethical muscles. Think of yourself operating with the highest integrity and ethics and that's the way you'll become. Every day watch your own behavior. Pat yourself on the back when you make decisions that support this new direction. Notice your lapses. Try to understand and empathize with that part of yourself struggling to stay completely honest.

***

It was easy for Bob to imagine situations that would challenge his determination to share credit for accomplishments and to leave the guerrilla tactics behind him. He'd always prepared for the company's biweekly staff meetings by "priming the pump" before the meeting and softening the opposition by providing incomplete data. He told me, "I'm imagining myself laying out all the facts and encouraging the contributions of two people, in particular, whom I've put down a lot in the past. I'm brainstorming with them till they come up with a workable idea." Mentally, he practiced being honestly persuasive in building support for the joint idea they developed. He imagined himself thinking through the issues and employing strong, substantive facts to convince his peers to his way of thinking. He imagined doing so in a group setting where they strived to reach consensus decisions.

***

G GRADUATE TO THE NEW BEHAVIOR.

Give others a chance to help you and learn from you. Talk through your decisions with your employees. Let them see you choose to act with integrity time and again, even when it's tough. Model this new behavior so that they, too, will be ethical in the way they work. Confront shaky integrity in your own employees with kindly explanations of other, better ways to accomplish whatever is required.

***

Bob knew that he'd have to let people know he was going to change. Otherwise they'd think he was being manipulative again. But he was reluctant to be so open and admit that he needed to change. Bob found the courage when he realized it took strength and high self-esteem to do this disclosing. At the next meeting with his department, Bob told his group how determined he was to change his behavior and how much he hoped their perception of him would shift as he cleaned up his actions. "I guess I've done things that make me look like I can't be trusted," he admitted. "And I want your respect."

———————

How do you feel about the importance of integrity in your daily work life now? Has your attitude shifted? Did the CHANGING Process help you see why you may have chosen less than honorable ways of behaving in the past? Did it help you recognize that you were less than totally caring toward yourself? Are you ready to be more ethical toward yourself and your employees? If so, you're ready to reap the rewards of a circle of trust.

PHASE TWO: BE A MODEL OF INTEGRITY AND TRUST IN YOUR MANAGEMENT STYLE

Operate with complete integrity as an individual and you are empowered to manage with integrity, too. In your immediate organization, whether it's a division, department, or team, you control opportunities and wield power that permit you to take responsibility for ethical business decisions. Once you accept that responsibility, you initiate a trusting environment where all people can do more and better work because they feel good about what they're doing.

STEP ONE: HOLD YOURSELF ACCOUNTABLE
FOR ETHICAL DECISIONS.

Just as you hold employees accountable for getting their work done on time, no excuses accepted, you can hold yourself accountable for making moral product and people decisions as a manager. Do so even though moral decisions are not clearly defined or required by your company culture. Your employees will be watching to see if you "walk your talk." They will notice the little decisions, particularly, because those often affect their day-to-day lives. Tom Peters urges, in *Thriving on Chaos*, "Do not make any commitment, starting right now, internal or external, that you can't live up to."

Gay Hendricks, psychologist, business consultant, and university professor, tells me that he pays a personal secretary to do all his book manuscript typing and that he does not use the university administrative staff or copying machine to reproduce articles for his book research. This is contrary to the behavior of most other faculty members. Hendricks explains, "It's simply not right for the school to pay for my typing and copying expenses unless I'm willing to sign over a portion of my book royalties to them."

What does it matter if we lack honor in the way we manage? Who does it hurt? The Worth Ethic cannot function in an atmosphere of suspicion and disrespect. When we misuse what's entrusted to us, we know what we've done and our employees suspect as much. They lose respect for us and our organization. Alternatively, great personal integrity supports our highest nature, so that we respect ourselves and those around us.

STEP TWO: OPERATE WITH AN EYE TOWARD FULL DISCLOSURE.

A good way to decide if a decision sufficiently meets your ethical standards is to ask yourself, "Am I willing to disclose my decision or action to my manager, my CEO, the board of directors, my family, friends, and society as a whole?" You may decide your competitors don't need to know your strategies, but if you cringe at the thought, you may be considering an unethical act. The old question, "Would you want your decision to appear on the front page of *The Wall Street Journal*?" still holds. You and your corporation may maintain that there's really no problem, but a personal survey of how many trivial actions you are reluctant to disclose might be instructive.

My personal guide is never to make any decision or do any behavior that I am not comfortable posting on my door at work and broadcasting to all my friends. We all make many, many decisions each year; inevitably, a great number of them have ethical implications. With most, we're clear what to do and the high path is an easy one. But occasionally the water is muddier. Disclosure is a way of sounding those submarine depths of conscience and examining our decisions.

Faced with an ethical dilemma, a "should I or shouldn't I" situation, ask yourself the following questions. Your answers will tell you whether your anticipated action is worthy or self-serving.

- *Am I likely to achieve what I'm after, long-term, going with this decision?*
- *How will others in the organization be affected by my decision?*
- *Will anyone or everyone in the organization support me?*
- *Who gets hurt by my decision?*
- *Whose rights, ultimately, am I most responsible for?*
- *How will my client or customer look at this decision?*
- *If my decision becomes public knowledge, how will I feel about it?*
- *Why am I making this decision?*

STEP THREE: OPERATE WITH HONESTY AND OPENNESS.

Trusting others is the reciprocal of being trustworthy. At KLA, once we scaled that twenty-foot wall together, the lessons we learned were taken back to work with us. We tried the same approach, risking first a little and then a lot. I found that when I was more self-disclosing, I encouraged my staff to trust me. Then, as my staff members went out of their way to keep me better informed about potential problems and looming deadlines, I developed greater trust in their capabilities.

Certainly, trust is at the heart of building a Worth Ethic environment. There is an ease and buoyancy about running an ethical company that comes when everyone behaves openly and honestly. Dr. Paul H. Schurr of the State University of New York at Albany and his colleagues tested the relationship between trust and cooperation. They found that in simulated sales negotiations a buyer who believes in the seller's trustworthiness makes more concessions. Will Schutz, San Francisco psychologist and business consultant, says that if people in companies told the truth, 80 to 90 percent of their problems would disappear. When we act with honor, we discover with Schutz that people are "relentlessly reasonable, cooperative, and capable of coming to sensible and productive agreements."

Moreover, the political maneuvers that haunt and handicap most organizations tend to disappear when we work openly and honestly. Free at last to tell the truth without reservation, we find it easy to banish misconceptions and suspicions. We find it simple to let our associates know what's going on and what they can do to help us. We find it invigorating to work without a smoke screen to impede our vision. In other words, when we are open and honest, we are more productive.

PHASE THREE: INSTILL HIGH ETHICAL STANDARDS WITHIN YOUR COMPANY

What can we do when we perceive that our company's ethics are at variance with our own ideals? We can play ostrich, hiding our heads in the sand. We can leave for a more compatible company culture. We can stay and stick it out, holding ourselves and our employees accountable for work decisions.

However, if we stay, we must instill our renewed integrity and build trust within the corporation at every opportunity. The CHANGING Process encouraged you to imagine new and more ethical ways of working. Now I'm going to show you how to *act* on your best intentions.

STEP ONE: URGE YOUR COMPANY TO WRITE A CODE
OF ETHICS OR STANDARDS OF CONDUCT.

We would all like to think our employees know right from wrong, and probably they do. Still, without implicit trust that the company will back them up, many employees will do the expedient thing in ambiguous or potentially disastrous situations. What do they tell a customer when a product won't be delivered on time? What recourse do they have if a manager gives them an unfair performance evaluation? What do they do if they suspect their boss is taking kickbacks?

To support their higher instincts, employees need something down in writing that tells them the appropriate, expected behavior in difficult situations. Begin where your employees are. Maybe your first action should be to let them know what's legal and what's illegal in your business. May they accept a gift from a customer? May they make political contributions from company funds? Is it acceptable to use a company car for private business?

Beyond the legalities, you need to address areas where judgment enters in. Can they accept lunch with a competitor? Is it appropriate to ask a secretary to make personal flight reservations, do personal typing, or pick out gifts for personal friends? If so, may they offer a gift to the secretary for doing these special favors? Should they share company-sensitive information such as sales figures or contract awards? Should they use airline mileage awards from work trips only for their business travel? You need to identify the kinds of ethical decisions they may face and let them know what choices they are expected to make.

Work with your group to help them think through and write their own ethical credo. This should be a straightforward statement of the group's ethical standards, the mechanisms it uses to resolve ethical issues, and the audits used on a daily basis to ensure the honor of the group and its work.

STEP TWO: SET UP MECHANISMS THAT ENSURE THAT THE
EXPECTATIONS AND OBJECTIVES ARE REALISTIC.

The ethical credo or standard of conduct will generate ethical behavior when you use the audits and employ the mechanisms that enforce them. Don't let employees see other people getting ahead by using unethical practices. Let them know where to complain and to v hom. Then be sure you follow through.

How do you expect employees to react when they are given an impossible job to do? They can work very hard of course. But, short of a miracle, the impossible is impossible unless they can locate extra resources. Where do they go for help? And is it all right to ask for it? Let them know what you expect them to do. Then follow through with the help they need. Otherwise they'll do the impossible the only way they can, and that may include cutting corners and caving in on integrity. Remember, a company that sets high standards of ethics without creating thoughtful ways to live by them dooms itself to an environment of distrust, suspicion, envy, and unproductiveness.

STEP THREE: BROADCAST YOUR HIGH EXPECTATIONS.

Let one or two managers do anything unethical, and employees will point to them as an excuse for their own behavior. Still, if you know what's going on, you have the power to stop "rot at the top." Be visible and vocal about your standards of business conduct.

Develop systematic programs and informal means of showing your respect for highly ethical employees. Publicize the little ways in which your company lives up to its standard of ethics. Give visibility to ethical behavior by promoting only managers and employees who are good role models for your group. If half your bright stars are a bit slimy around the edges, if they weasel their way through projects, step on other employees, or sucker customers even just a little, don't recognize their performance with promotions. If you do promote them, you're sending a powerful message to your employees that this is appropriate behavior, that this is what it takes to be a winner with you. In as many ways as you can, let people know you expect the group to work honorably.

You will develop grassroots support for your efforts when you help employees recognize ethical issues in business and understand the ethical standards of the company. On an informal basis, talk openly about the ethical dilemmas you face. Share with them the questioning process outlined earlier, so they can use it in their own decision making.

In formal training for employees, be sure these two questions are discussed: (1) In hindsight, were decisions made with integrity? (2) Did the decisions harm or help business, long-term? By encouraging your employees to discuss the ethics of decisions at work and training them to analyze the results of alternative decisions, you give them the tools to make honorable and practical decisions.

Formal training in managerial integrity should emphasize the advantages of investing time to think through ethical dilemmas. It makes sense to determine the probable effects of alternate decisions before any damage is done. Wherever possible, review actual ethical challenges from the recent past, ones that required ticklish decisions, and walk managers through the decision process. Another approach is to ask participants for descriptions of ethical dilemmas they've faced and discuss these situations as case studies. Or refer to Barbara Toffler's excellent book, *Tough Choices*. In it she describes a number of case studies posing ethical dilemmas for managers. Some of these studies may examine issues that are pertinent to your own company, yet seem less exposing than in-house examples. Finally, work a discussion of ethics into every other training program you provide, from performance evaluations to health and safety regulations.

3

MEANING IN WORK
Plugging Ordinary Tasks into Extraordinary Values

"People make and discover their own meaning."
—ROLLO MAY, *Love and Will.*

The musician tunes her instrument. The artist cleans his brushes. The parent polishes the baby's white shoes. Physicians and teachers, believing their life's work has inherent value, do not shirk from even the most tedious and trivial tasks that relate to their professions.

If, somehow, jobs more ordinary than these were invested with great meaning, ordinary people could draw satisfaction from work just as the musician, the artist, the parent, the doctor, and the teacher often do. Throughout my career I have seen secretaries take great personal satisfaction from their jobs by providing the glue for separate departments. Each one provides scheduling, word-processing, telephone, and administrative support for large groups of people. Hardly the kinds of tasks that win worldwide admiration or huge bonuses, but in addition the secretaries take personal responsibility to make their groups function, and function compassionately, in the face of canceled appointments, threatening deadlines, and emergencies. They calm the rattled manager who's about to make a scapegoat out of an innocent technician, and they listen to the disgruntled employee who's threatening to quit over an "average" performance review.

MEANING CREATES JOB SATISFACTION

Meaning in work is the emotional as opposed to the rational reason we work. It is the raw material with which we inspire ourselves, our employees, and our company to far greater satisfaction and productivity.

Workers in the new work force want to believe their work efforts contribute to society, and they insist that their contribution be acknowledged. They don't look at work as a way to raise cash or create profit for stockholders. They look at work as a social, nurturing, and creative outlet. As Daniel Yankelovich and John Innerwahr wrote in *Work in the 21st Century*, in previous generations, people worked to survive. Today, they are increasingly inclined to work as a means of self-expression. Job holders interviewed by Yankelovich and Innerwahr estimate that only 5 percent of their parents worked primarily for self-development, compared with 17 percent of workers today. Robert Schwartz, founder of the Tarrytown Executive Conference Center and the School for Entrepreneurs, estimates that at least 60 percent of people expect to see their highest ideals and dreams brought to life through their work.

More and more, people want to work in a high-autonomy environment. The new knowledge workers seek it out in high-technology and service-oriented companies, and we welcome their capabilities. We also see increasing numbers of reformed "yuppies" willingly cash in their $80,000 salaries for $40,000 positions that deliver more personal satisfaction. A 1988 survey by the *Personnel Journal* found 36 percent of personnel officers in one hundred corporations ranked job satisfaction over job security as the number one concern of workers today. What makes for job satisfaction? A connection between people's work tasks and their personal sense of purpose.

When readers of *Psychology Today* were asked the job aspects they found most satisfying, the first three rankings were, in order of importance: the chance to do something that makes you feel good about yourself as a person; the chance to accomplish something worthwhile; and the chance to learn new skills. In other words, they yearned for the Worth Ethic. Significantly, the amount of pay received ranked twelfth out of eighteen.

For the bulk of the new work force, the meaning in work may well become the meaning of life itself. Job satisfaction outranks job security by a two-to-one margin as the number one concern of workers today. Margaret Magnus, editor of *Personnel Journal,* reports that employees in the new work force expect more than wages and benefits. They expect work to provide them with personal fulfillment, social relationships, and connection to the community.

When our core values are connected to our job, work engages our minds and hearts as well as our bodies. Core values are nearly sacred to each of us. We yearn to keep stretching our imaginations, adding to our knowledge, bringing humor or delight, or harmony or happiness to the people who inhabit our worlds. Unfortunately, we are often unaware of these core values, which tend to lurk in our unconscious. I suspect that most people who are excited about their work are in jobs that connect to their core values, whether or not they consciously sought out such jobs. Such an alignment is clearly present, for example, in the tasks of the senior scientist whose joy in life is making new discoveries.

What about ordinary workers and ordinary jobs? I've already told you how the secretaries find meaning and satisfaction in their work. Similarly, the lead assemblers find satisfaction in taking their training responsibilities seriously, serving as coaches and friends to new workers under them. I know a garage attendant who sees himself as a missionary of happiness. For years, whenever I'm in San Francisco, I have parked in a particular garage run by Metro Park. The service is prompt and the attendant there is friendly and happy. Once I asked him what kept his smile so constant and he told me that he feels his job in life is to brighten up the tired and often grouchy people who park their cars in his garage. I know a coordinator of administrative support services who, when she hires a new receptionist, makes it clear that handling the switchboard and message center is a public relations as well as a service function. Recognizing this, the women quickly drop their stereotyped, computerized "good mornings" and substitute warm, cheery voices that tell callers that KLA is glad they called.

Contrast these attitudes with those of managers who think their own workday is spent in inconsequential paperwork and workers who see their job as a series of cut-and-dried tasks. Do they take satisfaction in manufacturing a perfect air hose, for instance? Hardly. If they did, quality control would not remain the manufacturing problem it is today.

But suppose that same air hose is used in hospital equipment that can save a child's life. If workers envision the final use of their product and see the difference it makes, they can feel real satisfaction in doing their job well. Interesting, isn't it, that the tasks remain the same in each case. The content of the work is the same. But the context has been transformed.

MEANING HAS A PROFIT IMPACT

Cramped vistas generate low levels of urgency and commitment. Fortunately, heroic goals create significant efforts. We are motivated and satisfied when our broad work goals connect to our fundamental personal values: to discover something new, to be helpful, to create beauty, to find excitement, to ignite others' efforts, to instill harmony, to integrate information into ideas. Similarly, on a broad scale we find meaning in work when we align our personal efforts of body, mind, and heart to the collective meanings of others who contribute to what we do. In this way, we see meaning in what we do together, as a corporation, and gain self-esteem from our contribution to the totality of what we make.

When people see a fundamental value to what they do, their frustration with the irksome and tedious aspects of their jobs dissolves. Like the athlete who runs laps out of sight of the roaring crowd, workers, too, come to see their efforts as the route to a worthy goal. They feel less annoyance and are less angry when things go wrong. The proposal-writing team reduced to assembling 100 copies of a 200-page document by hand, throughout the night, because the collater is down and the deadline is noon the next day, may be unhappy about the chore. But they do it without rancor.

"The first priority of business leadership is to create and utilize purpose," Lawrence M. Miller writes in *American Spirit*. A noble purpose creates self-motivated employees. In the creative, flexible environment preferred by the new work force, output relies on their commitment, not a supervisor's control. Working without direct supervision, the employees who want to slack off can easily do so, holding back and reserving their enthusiasm for after-hour activities. On the other hand, people who are committed to their work waste less time, are more productive, and consequently generate greater profit. Those profits translate to a higher standard of living for everyone associated with the company.

BLOCKS TO FINDING MEANING IN WORK

Find meaning in your work and you add satisfaction to your life, change the very context of work, even add to the productivity and profitability of your organization. Yet you hesitate to look for meaning in work. Why? Because of your fear, lack of interest, or perhaps an inability to do so.

YOU ARE AFRAID TO LOOK FOR MEANING IN WORK
FOR FEAR YOU WON'T FIND IT.

What is your purpose in life? Why are you here? This is an existential dilemma for most of us. Particularly when we are younger, before mid-life prompts us to delve into some of the deeper questions, we are apt to set aside these uncomfortable considerations. Suppose we fail to find any meaning in what we do. Do we then admit we're working to pay the bills? College-educated people invest a significant portion of their lives preparing for a career. But history majors who started out to discover the causes of war get waylaid into running car dealerships, and chemistry majors who thought they'd create a new energy compound end up developing household cleaners. The days turn into weeks, months, and years. And we wonder, with a cold chill, what if our work has no purpose?

YOU HAVE ALREADY CONNECTED TO A DEEP PURPOSE
IN LIFE OUTSIDE OF WORK.

Perhaps you lack interest in pursuing meaning in work because you're hooked into your core values elsewhere. Long ago, maybe as long ago as your school days, you got the idea that there were two parts to life—school and play. You saw school, and later work, as the effort you had to put out in order to meet your family obligations. You may have felt that you learned a lot of meaningless information in school and didn't do very well there, and that today you do a lot of meaningless tasks at work and don't do so well there either. Work is simply a means of supporting the activities and relationships you value, not an end in itself. Consequently, you look at play, recreation, and time with your family as the things that give real value to your life.

You are hardly alone in landing on that alternative. If we could mobilize some of the energy that people spend at home taking care of their gardens, tending to their bicycles, painting rooms, and so forth, and channel that initiative and momentum into the workplace to generate national productivity, what a tremendous difference it could make in all our lives.

YOUR WEEK-TO-WEEK ACTIVITIES NO LONGER INCLUDE OPPORTUNITIES TO LOOK FOR DEEPER MEANING.

In the past a community's churches and schools put a lot of emphasis on experiencing the spiritual side of life. The great majority of people went to church at least once a week and left services feeling inspired to do good in the world. School-children pledged allegiance to the flag and paused before their studies for a moment of prayer. Literature was selected and studied with an eye toward its moral lessons. School choruses sang sacred music and school classes put on Christmas plays and Easter pageants.

As more and more of our population has moved away from organized religion, and our schools, in an effort to be nonjudgmental and even-handed, stress skill development over values, nothing has appeared to provide substitute opportunities for inspiration. A popular saying in my own group of friends was, "Well, we can get as much from communing with nature as from going to church." But then the walks became jogs, the emphasis shifted to physical fitness, and spiritual connection fell by the wayside. What remains, still, is the unabated drive to achieve something special and a vague emptiness that cannot be filled either through our relationships with other people or through meaningless work.

YOU SIMPLY DON'T KNOW HOW TO LOOK FOR DEEPER MEANING IN YOUR LIFE.

I was in this dilemma in 1980 when I went to a powerful workshop taught by psychologist John Enright and author LaUna Huffines. The workshop was attended by a number of Silicon Valley engineers and technical managers, all of us seeking guidance on how to delve into our deeper personal meanings. John and LaUna suggested that we look back over our lives, all the way back to childhood, for events that stood out for us as times when we felt "in the flow" and deeply touched by what we were doing. They encouraged us to look for times when we were making a difference rather than winning public acclaim.

Then, after we made some notes to ourselves, we were encouraged to look for an umbrella that linked all of the events. In my own case, I found two different themes. One was the role of helper, the other was as a ground breaker. The first pattern showed up as early as the second grade for me. I remembered several instances of giving friends encouragement to try something far beyond what they thought possible. The second pattern began to emerge by the time I was ten and in the sixth grade. I remembered bringing in some new programs that became annual events for the next ten years.

Such umbrella themes are intrinsic to each of us. They reflect our self-images and are founded in our personal values systems. It's amazing how early we can begin to pick them out within ourselves. In the workshop with John and LaUna, I identified my core values and then we connected them to my present job by considering their ultimate impact on my daily activities.

PHASE ONE: FIND MEANING IN YOUR WORK

It's easy to feel overwhelmed by the amount of mundane, seemingly trivial work that we do, whether we're managers, engineers, assemblers, marketers, or service representatives. Do you feel much of what you do is wasted effort? Every job involves tasks that we've grown beyond. Such tasks simply aren't demanding or challenging any longer. In addition, parts of our jobs are just more exciting than others. So, sometimes we're bored and sometimes we're working at the highest level of excitement.

In your search for meaning in work, it's important to realize that meaning transcends challenge. You can find a clue to your core values when you analyze your present job, even if it no longer excites you. For example, people with a deep appreciation for harmonious relationships find meaning in boring jobs that permit them to work side by side with close friends. Meaning can transcend the work environment or the people with whom you work. Generations of students, working in cafeterias, canneries, and car washes to pay for the cost of college, have shown that.

Where do you find the deeper meaning of your work? The CHANGING Process can help you discover the lure that attracted you to your job in the first place, help you turn on to your job, and ultimately help your "turned-off" employees as well. I'll help the process along with some self-disclosure that I hope will lead you to examine your own job closely and to uncover possibilities for deeper meaning in your work.

C   CREATE A CONCRETE DESCRIPTION
OF THE DESIRED CHANGE.

Look carefully at the specific task for which you are striving to find meaning. Ask yourself what the task is supposed to accomplish at the most profound level. Specifically, identify your own doubts and disbeliefs about the significance of the work you are doing.

The first time I had serious doubts about the meaning of my work was in 1979. As a new manager of training and development for a consumer products company, my first assignment was to teach a program for employees that explained how performance evaluations were done, how jobs were coded and graded, and how the salary system was administered.

Boring, I thought. The material was the kind of stuff anyone would immediately tune out. I sat through one program and, long before the day ended, I knew I wouldn't like presenting something this analytical and repetitious. Nevertheless, that was my assignment.

I tried to fault the course by asking myself, "Is this program really useful?" But I kept getting this nagging feeling that, "Yes, it was." Nevertheless, I like working when I'm excited and motivated about what I'm doing, and this particular project seemed absolutely dull. So I dug around, looking for meaning. Because I honestly admired my manager, who had designed the program, I wouldn't let myself feel that he didn't know what he was doing. For the same reason, I squashed a mounting resentment that the company would spend its limited training dollars on such an uninspiring course. Instead, I focused on what possible meaning this program might have for me and for the class.

H   HONESTLY EXAMINE YOUR MOTIVATION TO CHANGE.

Nobody changes unless he or she wants to change. Get in touch with your real reasons for wanting to find more meaning in work.

In this situation, I was highly motivated because I didn't want to go on automatic pilot, doing a program month after month that not only bored the class, but bored me. This is not the way I like to work.

A   ABANDON THE OLD BEHAVIOR IN YOUR IMAGINATION.

Since your customary approach to your job leaves you feeling flat, like sparkling water left uncapped in the refrigerator, now's the time to imagine how your enthusiasm will revive when you discover meaning in your work.

In the past I would simply have taken that assignment and done the very best I could with it. If, on looking it over, I decided it was a reasonable program as structured, I would have done it the way it had always been done. Or—and this is more probable—I would have figured out how to lighten up the content, do better visual aids, and put some liveliness in the program.

This time, I imagined myself doing something far more important—finding a kernel of real meaning in the course. I thought about how thrilled I would feel presenting this significant information and how valuable and respected the course would become.

N   NAME THE CHANGE POSITIVELY.

Look carefully at this new you, committed to discovering meaning in your work. Then devise a couple of short sentences you can remember easily, to help you focus on your new attitude toward work.

For me the clearest statement was, "I find meaning and I am personally turned on about the value of this program."

G   GIVE ATTENTION TO PAYOFFS.

If you haven't found meaning in your work in the past, it's because you got certain payoffs for not looking for meaning, for accepting things as they were.

My biggest payoff was that, by not bucking the system and raising the issue of something as esoteric as the "meaning" or "value" of the course, I had one less battle to fight with myself. I was trying to avoid being as idealistic as I was in my twenties. I had a comfortable job. Wasn't that enough? Did everything have to have meaning? In addition, my workday went along more smoothly when everyone assumed I bought into my assignments without questioning their value.

I   IMAGINE THE PAST AND SEE HOW YOU BEHAVED.

Confront the work you did in the past and the absence of meaning in it. Think about how you would have approached your work tasks differently if you had seen the significance of what you did. Imagine how different you might be today if someone back then had helped you connect your work to your deepest values and innermost drives.

Looking back into the past, I could see that many times I had worked on projects with which I didn't feel personally connected. Sure, I did a good job, but not an outstanding one.

As I reviewed my past, I plugged into the idea: "What if I were excited because I really saw meaning in what I did?" I remembered my first job as a survey analyst in Saigon. At first, I felt the job had possibilities. Then I became discouraged by the working environment and began analyzing pieces of data and designing survey instruments without connecting those tasks to my original purpose in taking the job. What if I had been able to keep my original vision—that in some small way I was helping to create a peaceful environment in Vietnam? I would have felt exhilarated by what I was doing.

Next, I thought back to my days working on a large grant at the University of Texas, in which I analyzed educational programs for older people. There, too, I had begun a job feeling as if there was a real possibility of finding meaning in the work, but somehow that never really happened. So I thought about how I would have felt, and how much faster I would have found my life's purpose, if I had kept sight of the ultimate impact the research study might have.

_____

N   NAIL DOWN THE NEW BEHAVIOR
USING MENTAL REHEARSAL.

Look forward to upcoming work situations and imagine how you will persist until you uncover the inherent meaning in the work you are doing.

_____

In my case, I tackled the deadly dull procedural program I was supposed to present every month. I reflected on it for nearly three days as I drove to and from work. I kept asking, over and over, "What is significant about this program? What value does it bring to the people attending the course?"

In a flash, the answer occurred to me one evening. Because this program informed employees about how salaries correlated with level of responsibilities and education, how managers evaluated employee performance, and how salary increases were financed and justified, it gave people, most of whom were hourly workers, a new understanding of money. This was a part of their lives in which they almost never felt they had any power. If they understood how money is distributed, what it takes to make more money, and how to have useful discussions with their managers about their salaries, they would be less likely to be victimized by the system that paid them. And by providing this link, I would be working from my deepest purpose, that of helping others. The company would also benefit by having employees who were much less resentful about their pay.

With this bit of insight, I reconstructed the program slightly. I prefaced the first segment with questions connecting the policies and procedures to the employees' daily lives. I asked, "How many of you feel that you've been jerked around when salary increases were given? How many blamed your supervisor, or your supervisor's manager, or Personnel?" Almost everyone's hand shot up.

"What could you have done differently?" I asked. They didn't know. They felt like victims. So I asked them to make a commitment, that day, to get in charge of that part of their lives. We discussed strategies for taking charge, such as having more information and identifying the key decision makers. At that point, they were ready to listen to the information I'd come to deliver.

For the remainder of the course, I used the same basic materials used in previous classes. But I kept reminding the class that the information I was sharing would help them understand and control the money aspects of their lives. I concluded each segment with strategies they could use to put their new knowledge to work for them. One person admitted she was surprised by a poor performance review, because she hadn't known what was expected of her. We came up with questions she could ask her manager, so she'd never again be taken by surprise like that. We talked about negative feedback and how to make sure that managers saw and acknowledged specific performance improvement. The information was practical, personal, and clearly related to their paychecks.

At the end of my first presentation, three of the fifteen attendees told me that they felt their lives had been completely changed by this "procedural" course. I was moved by their enthusiasm, and a potentially boring work assignment began to have real meaning for me, too. The program in time became very popular, and the experience taught me the power that comes from connecting an ordinary task to an extraordinary meaning in work.

G GRADUATE TO THE NEW BEHAVIOR.

Now it is time for you to help others learn from you. You need to share your own insights so that your employees and peers understand the significance of uncovering the meaning in their everyday work.

I had no trouble talking about my profound success with the "procedural" training program. Certainly I shared my changed viewpoint with the immediate and succeeding classes, and subsequently with various departments I managed over the years.

Today I look for meaning in all areas of my work. For example, take compensation. For years I avoided taking on compensation responsibilities because I dislike number crunching. It reminds me too much of my days as an engineer. I felt compensation was far removed from the heart of the company until, at KLA, I realized that if a company does not reward people who give it what it wants, it doesn't get it. I realized that compensation was a way to reinforce all the attitudes I value. Once I found meaning in this area, I became nearly obsessed with it. At one point, for about a year, compensation tasks dominated almost one-quarter of my workday.

PHASE TWO: MANAGE WITH MEANING

As a manager who recognizes the significance of finding meaning in work, how can you help employees connect ordinary jobs to extraordinary meanings? Sometimes, it looks so easy. The company nurse, for instance, should feel connected to the higher goal of maintaining people's health. But the person filling that job may not, at this particular moment, feel the job is important. A whole company may be set up in the hope of discovering a cure for AIDS or engineering a landing on Mars. Nevertheless, at least some employees will feel unconnected to the higher purpose of the company, be dissatisfied, and delivery shoddy workmanship.

The significance of a job depends on the employee's interpretation. Working for a defense company may mean making armaments or it may mean helping to keep America safe, depending on how a person looks at it. Meaning results only when someone makes a solid connection between fundamental internal drives and job tasks. To do so, follow these steps:

STEP ONE: SHARE YOUR OWN VISION OF MEANING IN WORK.

Not everyone will agree with your personal vision. Indeed, yours may change as you mature in your career. But with this step you begin to build an awareness of the value of finding deeper meaning in work. Explain how trivial or irksome chores have lost their power to aggravate or irritate you. Tell people about your new sense of purpose, your enthusiasm and dedication since you've hooked your work into your core values.

STEP TWO: TELL YOUR EMPLOYEES HOW YOU
UNCOVERED YOUR CORE VALUES.

Perhaps you got in touch with what your own life is about by looking inside and seeing what propels you. If you used the CHANGING Process, you must have searched your memory for the events that stand out. These may be events no one else even noticed, but of which you felt personally proud.

For me, one such event was saving my milk money in second grade. This is something indelibly imprinted on my memory. I saved my money so I could anonymously buy a ticket and donate it to a girl in our class who never attended any of the special events. Her parents couldn't afford the extra few dollars, and I chose to help them out, even at that young age. As I grew older this generic theme of helping out became more focused on helping along people who had shut down their feelings.

Now, as I look at myself, I see that one purpose of my life is to create compassion, to help people experience their feeling sides, not necessarily through social services, but in everyday ways. I shared with my staff the introspective steps I had to take to reach down to the roots of my own profound job satisfaction.

STEP THREE: DRAW PEOPLE'S ATTENTION TO THE TIMES WHEN THEY LOVE THEIR WORK.

Once your employees begin to think about it, they can probably relate that joy to their own core values. When Heidi Henderson, my secretary, first came to KLA as a temporary, I discovered that she had helped three runaway teenagers return to their homes, two to remote states. Over the last three years, I have seen that her life is very much about lending a hand. Heidi is the one person in the company who always knows if a young, single parent can't afford Christmas gifts for the kids. And she makes sure that person gets some help and support before December 25th. Whenever I see her take someone else's troubles on herself, locate the right resources, and get the person in touch with good help in a hurry, I remind her that it's not surprising she ended up working in human resources. Here, we're able to put her in a circumstance that enhances her fundamental purpose in life.

I often ask employees who report to me what they really loved doing that week. Then I listen. They hear, as I do, what their core values are. It takes only a few moments more to help them make the connection between what they love to do and why they love to do it.

STEP FOUR: DELINEATE CLEARLY BETWEEN LOVING YOUR WORK AND BEING A WORKAHOLIC.

Marilyn Ferguson, in *The Aquarian Conspiracy*, observes that for the workaholic, work is an addiction: "The workaholic, like an alcoholic, is indiscriminate in his compulsion." Like all addicts, the workaholic is numb to the pain of a life that doesn't work well, that brings little satisfaction. To find meaning in work is quite different from trying to find meaning by blindly working more hours for less satisfaction.

PHASE THREE: INSTILL A HIGH SENSE OF PURPOSE IN THE ENTIRE COMPANY

In *American Spirit*, Lawrence M. Miller warns that democratic capitalism has lost its spirit to invoke loyalty because it makes prosperity sound "merely materialistic." The reason, Miller says, is that we have forgotten how to inspire. The trick is to turn the dry company mission or vision statement into a brilliant beacon. Make the goal worthy and the work will become worthy, too. This is not a complicated process. It's as simple as reminding people of the end results of their labor. Employees already know their own roles. They know their own contributions to the work task. But they need to see the picture on the cover of the puzzle box to see where their piece fits in.

STEP ONE: IDENTIFY WITH THE HOPES AND DREAMS OF ORDINARY PEOPLE IN THE COMPANY.

To share the mission and vision of the company effectively, the purpose must be appealing. Before you begin to write a mission or vision statement, figure out how the company's products and services relate to common values. Do they make the world healthier, happier, safer?

Be sure to consult other managers and employees for their input. Together, think about the broader accomplishments in what you do at work. Remember the workers in the weapons industry: It isn't what you do, but how you look at it. A computer can control a Star Wars defense system or release handicapped people from the prison of their useless muscles.

One of the reasons KLA has been so successful, I think, is that the larger purpose of the company is so apparent to our employees. Our goal is to push back technical boundaries in the semiconductor industry and subsequently create products that were never before possible. If you are in charge of a plant that manufactures canned peaches, your mission may not be so obvious. On the other hand, you can still identify the greater meaning of your particular endeavor: to deliver the highest quality food, perhaps, or to develop the most efficient system possible, while still supporting employees, so that you control your final cost to the customer.

General Electric's John F. Welch has used "ownership" as a corporate theme for almost seven years. In 1988, he shifted to "liberation" because he wanted employees to take charge of their actions. It's true that the word "ownership" implied the freedom to act. But employees further down in the organization didn't get the message. Now, Welch says, he can ask them, "Are you free to do things? Is your job more exciting, more challenging, than it was a year ago or two years ago?" Those questions are easier to understand than, "Do you feel ownership?"

STEP TWO: DEVELOP A MISSION OR VISION STATEMENT
THAT CHARTS YOUR COMPANY'S DIRECTION.

The mission statement concentrates on doing well at the business the company is in, the vision statement on doing well because of the business the company is in. For example, McDonald's fundamental mission is to stay highly profitable. Its vision is "the gospel of quality, service, cleanliness, and value." Should your company focus on its mission or its vision? You'll find much literature and many advocates for each approach, and the distinction is beyond the scope of this discussion. Fundamentally, however, the difference is time.

Develop a mission statement when you are concerned about the upcoming two years. With a turnaround situation, a new merger, or a rapidly changing marketplace, the company has immediate problems to solve. The mission statement is appropriate. The vision statement is about the next six to sixty years. In stable situations where less structural change is going on, the company can look farther out and identify with an ultimate vision of change and contribution to society.

A year ago we did some brainstorming in KLA's human resources department. After a number of collaborative meetings, we were clear on our objective: to turn every employee of the company into a human resources "customer." We wanted to create an environment for our customers that would help KLA optimize its profits. We didn't create a fancy document, mind you. We wrote up a very real goal that has managed to invest even the computerizing of our benefits system with a sense of mission. And vision.

Suppose your executive office decides that the goal of the company is to grow 20 percent next year. What kind of vigor can you generate with numbers? Financial targets are worthy objectives, but they lack the emotional impact of people-oriented goals. Instead, choose a mission, such as providing high-quality customer service or leading-edge products. These are missions that employees can relate to. If customers are well satisfied with what your company does, profits will follow. Meanwhile, it's a lot easier for people to get thrilled over a letter from a satisfied customer than a dry statistic.

At GE, Welch says he wants to get closer to the individual—the source of the creative energy that the company needs. The fewer levels of management the company has, the greater the number of people who report to each manager. This change had three results for GE: managers concentrated on key decision making rather than nitpicking; the "star performers" had more visibility; and the company has already saved $40 million in administrative costs. But GE mentions the dollar savings only as a way of quantifying its success.

STEP THREE: BROADCAST THE MISSION OR VISION.

Make the statement the rallying point for the recruitment and marketing efforts of the company. In your newsletter, tell stories about employees who personify your mission or vision. Consult the statement and use it as a guide when you do office layouts, create employee perks, decide on celebration themes, or anything else that affects and affirms your company culture.

On a regular basis, point out how people's jobs connect to the company's goal. Especially at first, people will not necessarily do this themselves. Make the connection in every meeting you hold. Without this link, people stop believing the mission or vision statement has any personal significance for them. Then it becomes a piece of promotional material that "somebody upstairs" developed, not anything that helps them find meaning in what they do.

There's a new management process at GE that substitutes for having managers report to corporate staff executives. Company managers meet to talk about their respective businesses, share their problems, and outline their business opportunities. Welch says the test of a person's success as a manager, in these meetings, is this: "Are you boring anybody else in there? That's literally the test of the meeting—have you got new ideas that can excite other people?" Welch wants even lower-level managers to agitate for the freedom to do better, more creative work. He says, "We now have an even greater and simpler test for people. They can look at their boss and say, 'Hey, I'm doing stuff that [top management] says I shouldn't be doing. I'm working eleven hours a day, I'm not having fun, I'm still filling out vouchers, and [top management] tells me I shouldn't be doing that. Why are you making me?' "

When your company gets in touch with its deepest purposes, the practice of developing a company mission or vision statement becomes an uncommon Worth Ethic tool. For example, the manufacturing segment of the computer industry set out to revolutionize the way people work. That was its vision. Its more immediate mission was to make computerized machines so effective and easy to operate that companies would be willing to invest in them. With exciting, customer-oriented goals like that, the people at Apple Computer, Sun Micro-systems, and KLA Instruments go about their tasks with exhil-aration and dedication. Like the musician, the artist, the parent, the physician, and the teacher, they connect the neces-sary chores to the core meaning of their work.

4

PERSONAL POWER
Sharing Control Earns High Dividends

Never take advantage of power.
Achieve results, but never glory in them.
Achieve results, but never boast.
Achieve results, but never be proud.
Achieve results, because this is the natural way.
Achieve results, but not through violence.
Force is followed by loss of strength.
—LAO TSU, *Tao Te Ching*

At the National Bank of Chicago, the 110-person department responsible for issuing letters of credit was a paper mill, riddled with fragmented tasks. Then, working as a team, the department's managers and employees restructured it to integrate the low-level, unrewarding jobs into positions with a degree of personal power. They designed a new job classification called "documentary products professional," which required upgraded skills and offered a 20 percent salary increase. The bank provided the necessary retraining, and within a year could report greatly improved productivity, customer satisfaction, employee job satisfaction, and increased unit profitability, even with the increased salary costs.

People in the new work force want work that acknowledges they can handle authority, and make worthwhile contributions; they want the right to see exactly how they contribute to the company's success. It is up to us managers to provide

that new kind of work—work that lets people make a difference.

If trust is the foundation on which you build the Worth
Ethic, aspects of personal power are the bricks used to create
an immediate difference in your organization. As a manager,
you have power and your employees want you to share it. It's
exciting to feel you personally make a difference. Your
employees, too, yearn for that same kind of satisfaction. This
means personal power, like the trust on which it's founded,
must be distributed throughout the organization.

You may be reluctant to share whatever hard-won power
you now have as a manager. But look what happens when you
do: Shenandoah Life restructured customer service jobs so that
workers operated on their own throughout the entire customer
service process, and call response time dropped astoundingly,
from twenty-seven to two days.

At the FBI, when job control was returned to workers and
performance expectations were raised in a demoralized sixty-
person support group, employee production increased 60 percent, a five-year backlog dropped by 50 percent, and morale
zoomed. At Frito-Lay, in a new 300-employee plant in California, management set up open systems of small teams of
workers. These teams were given final approval over new team
members, and they were asked to confer among themselves to
set production goals, to monitor quality, and to inspect what
they produced. Early results included saving over $30 million,
inspiring employee attendance of 99 percent, using 35 percent
fewer managers, and reaching full production not in the usual
six to thirteen weeks, but in one week flat.

This high level of success occurs frequently at manufacturing plants when employees are allowed to make a difference.
After management at General Motors' Tarrytown, New York,
plant received numerous complaints about leaky windshields,
they consulted the shift of welders whose windshields never
leaked. Those welders told them they added an extra amount
of adhesive at the windshield bottom. This quick solution
prompted management to consult other workers on other

kinds of problems. GM attributes its subsequent turnaround to this kind of collaborative effort in which employees are empowered to solve problems on their own. At the GM plant, absenteeism dropped from 7 percent to one percent, labor grievances dropped from 2,000 to 20, and the percentage of bad welds dropped from 35 percent to 1.5 percent.

What's going on here? When managers allow workers to play an active part in managing how they work, managers see their organization's quality, productivity and profitability go up. The essence of empowerment is sharing your managerial power to create a productive partnership with your employees. Let employees take part in decision making, make identifiable contributions, and share some of the credit, and they stop releasing poor quality products and services that disappoint consumers. In the end, you raise their effectiveness and their self-worth simply because you empower them to fix problems themselves.

Ralph McLaughlin, Director of Corporate Quality at Silicon Graphics, Mountain View, California, introduced a similar system of teamwork when he joined the company. Within four months, yield increased by 15 percent, the Material Review Board's number of rejects slid downhill, and the Disk Drive Improvement Team revised the manufacturing process, reducing required time to fourteen hours per product, down from thirty-six to forty hours. One day a team member overheard an OEM representative say he would accept a monitor even though it had a scratch on it. "Oh, no, you won't!" the employee objected. "We're working on that problem right now. That monitor doesn't meet company standards."

Employees who are asked to make things better make investments in the decisions that result. They pitch in to make the decisions work. Jim Kouzes and Barry Posner say in *The Leadership Challenge* that esprit de corps climbs right along with the workers' perception that a manager is encouraging collaboration and honestly relinquishing a measure of control and power over what they do at work.

BLOCKS TO EMPOWERMENT

I've told you of the successes that come from empowering employees but not the failures. Organizational Dynamics polled executives and found that while 95 percent agreed that letting workers decide quality issues would help tremendously in eliminating quality deficiencies, 58 percent don't act on that belief. Why not?

Three obstacles may stand between you, as a manager, and any serious attempt to reap the quality, job satisfaction, and productivity benefits of letting employees make a real difference at work. These obstacles revolve around issues of power, trust, and control.

YOU DON'T WANT TO SHARE YOUR POWER.

You've worked hard to get where you are today. No wonder you hesitate to delegate any serious responsibility to those who work for you. You dread the thought of depending on a peer, since he or she is a likely competitor for promotion. You feel that power is a limited resource, like diamonds, hard to get and senseless to cut into small pieces.

Often our concept of personal worth is tightly tied to being in charge. Even when we appear to seek cooperation and participation in a meeting, by asking people for their ideas, we're hoping, deep down, they'll come up with our idea. We may go so far as to rig the results by shooting down every idea but our own. Especially under pressure, we're likely to revert to dictating rather than working collaboratively. And since people are more likely to do our bidding in a crisis, we may deliberately procrastinate on a project until a critical deadline looms.

High achievers, in particular, often find themselves unable to share power. That's all right, as long as they work as independent sales people, design engineers, or copywriters.

They can succeed without building either commitment from those below or influence with those above them in the organization. Their concentration on self-interest rather than shared goals, doesn't necessarily impede their success.

Conversely, as a manager, you have to give some portion of your power away, since you cannot succeed independently—you must rely on others' efforts. Somehow you must build strong commitments from those who work for you. This means attracting capable people, making them feel capable, and treating them as capable. It means delegating authority to them to make key decisions without checking with you. It means giving them power of their own.

Managers succeed by attracting high-potential employees. Stars want to work for managers who can get the resources and go-aheads to make everyone shine. That means you have to develop broad influence throughout the company, something that takes time and energy not available to you when you spend all your time supervising employees. In short, if you are reluctant to share your personal power, you will ultimately lose it. You will be unable to attract and keep top quality employees, and you will subsequently fail. Managers who don't manage well plateau early in their careers or even lose their jobs.

Do you insist that your people follow the chain of command that now lets you control projects, decisions, even the flow of information in your organization? Continue to do so and you will never be able to move away from a supervising role into a leadership role. In the more than 500 cases reported in *The Leadership Challenge,* Jim Kouzes and Barry Posner did not come across a single example of excellent achievement without contributions from many people.

YOU WANT TO PLEASE EVERYBODY.

At the very opposite extreme from the rude, roughshod high achievers are the nice guys who want everybody to love them. These managers expect to convince themselves with their own popularity that they are lovable and worth loving. Their low self-esteem can never be bolstered from the outside; instead they need to learn how to love themselves first, from the inside.

These managers don't trust the company to acknowledge that tough decisions sometimes have to be made. They don't trust their fellow managers to recognize their valid contributions to the organization's success. They don't trust their own people to work hard and deliver good work. So they try to get everyone to love them in the unlikely hope that people will tolerate their lack of judgment out of affection.

If you have a need to be perennially popular, you won't do well at leading the new work force. Let's be realistic. Without self-worth you don't dare share your personal power. When you delegate responsibility to people under you, you invite them to stretch to meet your high standards. You put psychological pressure on them to perform well. You put yourself in the position of having to confront them, at times, with information they don't want to hear. But you will inspire them to new heights of achievement and new levels of confidence by giving them the power to try and the room to fail. And you won't always be popular—you may not even be liked, at least short-term.

Imbued with the Worth Ethic, the new work force expects to have a manager they can respect. They want a champion who's able to give them what they need: vision, guidance, encouragement, space, resources, budget, and top management support. In the end, given that kind of leadership, they will love their manager. It's a dichotomy: If you don't worry about keeping their affection, you'll get it in unending measure.

YOU DON'T HAVE THE NECESSARY LEADERSHIP SKILLS.

It's safe to say that having good leadership skills accounts for 85 percent of a manager's success in business. When the Carnegie Institute of Technology analyzed the records of

10,000 people, it concluded that 15 percent of success comes from technical skill on the job and 85 percent from the ability to deal successfully with people.

When Purdue University analyzed the records of its engineering graduates over a five-year period, it discovered that the graduates with the highest grades earned only $200 more per year than those with the lowest grades, but that graduates with notable social skills earned 15 percent more than the graduates with high grades and 33 percent more than those with low social ratings. The Bureau of Vocational Guidance at Harvard found that at least two-thirds of the people who lose their jobs do so not because they can't do the work, but because of their inability to deal with people.

Underdeveloped skills in listening to people, responding to them, and facilitating and integrating their ideas limit your personal worth as a leader. Dave Ferrise, a gifted technologist at Silicon Graphics, Mountain View, California, was intent on becoming an equally talented leader. When I began to work with him, he confided, "I used to think being smart was enough, that anyone who was sharp, by definition, could lead his group. Now I'm beginning to see that good leaders have a whole separate set of skills that they use to empower employees to produce more than they ever believed they could."

You probably abandoned attempts to shove your ideas down employees' throats. In fact, because of these past experiences, you probably think that you have asked for input on problems and that you do take time out to hear employees' ideas. You probably don't realize there's room for improvement. Do you serve as the filter and implementor of their ideas and receive the praise and rewards, too, if their ideas work? Most managers employ this middle-of-the-road approach to delegating power, thus denying employees any real chance to see how they make a difference.

In hundreds of employee exit interviews over the years, I've heard one primary complaint: Managers are unreceptive to employees' ideas. Employees, once they bump up against that, eventually stop looking for ways to improve the way they work. To let people see they've made a difference at work, you have to share the credit for good ideas and share the personal power to implement them.

Do you recognize some of your own behavior here? If so, it's time to recognize the difference between what was formerly required of a "boss," a person who supervised, criticized, and penalized, and what's looked for in a "leader," a peer or manager who, regardless of the external authority held, is expected to support, guide, and empower the group's ideas.

The role of employees, too, is changing. With fewer managers and flatter organization charts, employees are often expected to lead workgroups and projects. They are expected to lead, but do not necessarily know how to initiate, acquire resources, listen, confront, be persuaded, or praise helpers. Employees need these important skills and one way to develop them is to provide leadership training for the entire work group. But first they must see you, as a manager, modeling a high commitment to this new idea of sharing personal power.

PHASE ONE: WORK THROUGH THE CHANGING PROCESS

Managers who are achievement oriented, and that's most of us, work too hard and cherish too dearly the rewards of success to feel good about changing what seems to have worked for us in the past. It's true that we need to be more of a "leader" and less of a "boss." We see the wisdom of Marilyn Ferguson's dictum in *The Aquarian Conspiracy*, "You are only truly liberated when you liberate others."

But we can't seem to act on that wisdom. To untangle the roots of this reluctance, we're going to go through the CHANGING Process together.

C   CREATE A CONCRETE DESCRIPTION
OF THE DESIRED CHANGE.

Maybe you don't involve your people in decisions they should be part of. Perhaps you prefer to go it alone—you may feel it takes too long to involve others. Or maybe you're not such a good listener and you turn people off with your everlasting interruptions.

At age 35, Sam Kowalski already had a master's degree from M.I.T., a Ph.D. from the University of Illinois with a specialty in software engineering, a number of published articles to his credit, and experience heading up a forty-person group within a $400 million company. He was recruited out of this position into a smaller company about nine months before I was asked to work with him. Top management at the new company saw that Sam had high potential, but they perceived what might be a fatal flaw: Sam refused to let go of control. For example, he insisted on approving every financial decision over $200 for his group of 120 people, even though the people who reported to him had signature approval for $2,500. These were seasoned first-level managers, most of them older than he was.

On paper, Sam's title and responsibilities at the new company duplicated those at the old company. In reality, the challenge was significant: Sam needed to be the leader and role model for this large work group of experienced professionals; instead he had trapped himself by directing details and doing a great deal of the work himself.

During our first meeting, Sam charmed me with his "nice guy" style. He genuinely believed that he was participative, not particularly autocratic in style, and was setting a good example for his work group to follow. "I can't help it if I want to get involved. I love software development," he told me, "and I hate to let sloppy work go out of my shop."

As I interviewed the people who reported to him, over

the next week, I got a different picture. These people were very frank. "I get the feeling he doesn't trust me," one person said. Another complained, "It seems like he's right there at my shoulder all the time. He tells me exactly what to do and expects me to execute his ideas. I'm no longer allowed to think or to lead. It's not surprising that work isn't fun for me anymore." Sam had to let go of control and become a participative manager or his group of highly skilled technical people were going to abandon him for more satisfying situations.

H HONESTLY EXAMINE YOUR MOTIVATION TO CHANGE.

How much do you want to change? How important do you believe it is that you change this characteristic?

In Sam's case, the motivation to change was high. In three more months, he'd have a year in the job and he was still routinely working seventy-five hours a week. His family was upset. He knew he needed to delegate more work, yet he didn't feel comfortable doing it.

Most frustrating to Sam was the fact that he had no sense of what he could do to change his situation and himself. The people who worked for him had been rated mostly two and three on a five-point performance system by their previous manager. Sam thought that was correct. None of them seemed outstanding in the way he'd always been in his career. They didn't measure up to his standards of technical excellence. Still, he had to admit they were working in a group far larger than any he'd ever been in himself. And they all had project leaders reporting to them who were mostly Ph.D.s. Why couldn't he put his trust in them? Sam admitted he was ready to find out.

A   ABANDON THE OLD BEHAVIOR IN YOUR IMAGINATION.

What would your work style be like if you let your employees take an active part in managing how they work? This step will help pull you toward the change you are striving to attain.

Sam had no trouble imagining how he'd behave if he trusted his work group more than he did. He would do far more listening and far less directing. The people who worked for him would be more receptive to his input when they weren't feeling coerced into accepting his ideas. He thought that if he reshaped his role to lead rather than control these people, they would feel more ownership of the software designs they developed. They'd work harder, and maybe he could work less hard on the day-to-day stuff.

Sam liked the new organization that emerged in his imagination. He imagined ways of managing that would let him see the real capabilities of his group—he'd give his people more opportunities to show good judgment and make decisions on their own, let them know he could tolerate a few mistakes along the way, and develop his own skills in participative management. He'd be able to channel his energies into setting up new systems that would allow him to delegate with confidence and build a strong support network outside his group.

N   NAME THE CHANGE POSITIVELY.

For example, you might say, "I am a good listener." Or, "I encourage my employees to make decisions and always ask for their input before making decisions that affect the work group."

Sam said to himself, "I like being a participative manager. I trust my engineers and managers to make good decisions."

_____

G   GIVE ATTENTION TO PAYOFFS.

What advantage or reward came out of your reluctance to share personal power? For example, one way to control a meeting is to talk a lot, to contribute your ideas and occupy center stage. If you have used poor listening as a means to control, you've no doubt forced your ideas on someone else simply because you out-talked them.

_____

As Sam sorted through his past, he saw a lot of payoffs from his high-control behavior as long as he was working with small groups of no more than twelve to fifteen people. In high school, his good looks and easy manner made it easy to handle the lab partnerships and baseball teams he led. Everyone admired his ability to get the work done without last minute hassles.

Even in his early work assignments Sam won his managers' admiration for tracking costs and keeping to schedule on any small project he headed. Naturally, Sam felt the stretch when his job responsibilities broadened to managing thirty people. Still, by putting in a few extra hours a day, he could continue to create some of the software designs himself. The creative challenges and satisfaction that come from doing work he loved were still there for him.

Taking a critical look at his present situation, Sam told me, "I can see that the designs the group is turning out are not what I would have done, and I'm not at all sure their designs are as good or better than what I would have done. My managers are unhappy; I'm unhappy. I've lost control of the situation, and that's the one thing I always felt I was good at." With 120 people to manage, Sam's frustration and workload were poor payoffs for a career of hard work.

I IMAGINE THE PAST AND SEE HOW YOU BEHAVED.

Try to figure out why you behaved as you did in the past.
Suppose, for example, that you are one of those people who
doesn't listen. When you were a child, did you learn that you
never had a chance to add your say if you listened, that someone
would always interrupt you when you spoke? Or perhaps you
hate group meetings. Have you created problems in your career
and personal life by not showing up when you should have?

The glow Sam felt when he thought back to his early
successes faded when he imagined how much easier his life
could have been and how much less resentment he could have
caused over the years. He literally squirmed as he thought
back to a girl everyone called "the late, great Annie." Annie
was extremely creative at science projects, but she never finished anything until the last minute. Sometimes she missed
deadlines because of her enthusiasm to perfect her projects.

Throughout high school Sam had tried to get Annie to
work with him on a major science fair project. They'd have
been terrific together, but she refused. She didn't think she'd
like the strict schedules and formal meetings Sam had a reputa-
tion for using, even then. Sam thought about doing a project in
a looser atmosphere, giving Annie a chance to make a contribution, building something really outstanding.

But Sam wasn't sure a participative style was possible back
then. His parents had divorced when he was twelve, and that
made him the "little man" of his mother's life. "I did the
laundry. I made out the grocery list. I put the clean dishes in
the cabinets and stacked the dirty ones in the dishwasher. My
mom depended on me," Sam explained. These are responsibilities lots of children take on at home, but Sam took them
seriously. With my prompting, Sam imagined doing the work
but recognizing that his mother had final responsibility for how

well the apartment functioned. He imagined that he accepted his friends' offers to help out with the chores, on occasion. This was something he'd never done, even as an adult. Sam said to me, "You know, this urge to keep control showed up everywhere in my life, didn't it?"

He carried the control pattern into his marriage and held on to the family checkbook. "I like to reorganize the refrigerator, too," Sam admitted sheepishly. Sam thought about the vigorous arguments he had with his wife when they moved to their first house. He imagined cooperating with her instead of controlling every decision. He imagined her contented smile, as he worked with her to set up the kitchen cupboards and arrange the furniture.

Sam imagined that his work group had finished the Krouse Industries project on time. In reality, it had been stalled for six months because other projects had higher priority. Was this the beginning of a trend? Sam imagined that he had brought in all his managers to brainstorm the design concept and then parceled out responsibility for thinking through each approach. He imagined inviting the lead engineer to join them when they met to decide on the final design concept. The engineer alerted them to several manufacturing problems that later emerged. He imagined that he urged the group to discuss scheduling and deadlines before they committed to the ones they finally adopted. Using this scenario, he could easily imagine less resistance and less resentment within his work group. He could also imagine the relief of attending all subsequent meetings without running them himself.

**N   NAIL DOWN THE NEW BEHAVIOR
USING MENTAL REHEARSAL.**

Imagine the changed you that would have been created if you'd been encouraged to express yourself, to delight your listeners, and in turn had discovered that you learn more from listening than from talking. Refine your vision of how you want to be and now imagine yourself as this new person, this superb listener who is able to lead a group to all sorts of creative solutions to complicated problems, just by asking penetrating questions and then listening.

———————

Going forward in time, could Sam change the patterns of a lifetime and solicit and accept help from someone else? He needed to trust his employees to come through for him, yet he was embarrassed to realize how frustrated they must have been by his high-control management practices. Nevertheless, Sam mentally rehearsed his role as an accomplished participative manager.

Sam imagined he called a meeting in which he dispensed responsibilities for a new project. He encouraged each person to bid for the task he or she wanted to take on rather than passing them out, like assignments, as he would have done before. "This feels good," Sam admitted. "I feel more at ease and less stressed when I think about approaching the project this way."

Then he imagined how he would react during the next family confrontation. It was almost time to plan the summer vacation, and Sam imagined telling his wife what their budget could afford, then turning over the planning to her. She could pick the destination this time and deal with the troublesome details, too. Sam imagined his wife calling the travel agency, being put on "hold," and coordinating the details that always took him six or eight hours of work. He felt this way he could approach the vacation more relaxed and eager to have fun.

———————

G   GRADUATE TO THE NEW BEHAVIOR.

Set an example for your people. Encourage them. Let them know it's all right to ask for input and to spend time laying the groundwork to work collaboratively.

Sam and I worked together on a plan to let him become a more participative manager. His first action was to restore signature authority to his managers. Next Sam committed to take several training programs on interpersonal communication and meeting skills. We made a list of the new systems he would need. For example, he needed to set up routine team meetings, design reviews, and tracking mechanisms to be sure project milestones were being met. Finally, Sam shared his plans with the managers who worked for him and asked their help in finding more ways to let go. At our last session, armed with his plans, Sam said, "You know, Kate, one reason I feel so good about these plans is that they give me—you guessed it— some control." Sam grinned as he left my office.

PHASE TWO: MANAGE BY SHARING POWER

You let employees make a real difference in productivity when you solicit their ideas. Every time KLA considers introducing a new product, the design engineering group calls a meeting, inviting all key people in the company and plenty of senior engineers. The idea is to forestall any attempt that's been tried and failed, to abandon any effort that's unworkable, or—and this is always what's hoped for—to reassure ourselves that the path we're following is the best one possible. Senior level managers are present to assure their involvement and support, yet the engineers and managers have the power to make the final decisions.

I remember one time in particular when an engineering group was feeling frustrated during the final design clean-up of an exceptionally complex product, one that ultimately became the first of its kind ever delivered to computer chip manufacturers by any company. To get people involved in the problem, we took two different actions. First, we sent engineers to customer sites to talk with the people who were using the first version of the machines. Second, when customers came in for demonstrations, engineers were assigned to talk with them. In this way the engineers became important information conduits and also learned, first hand, the exact requirements and reactions of the customers. They gained a feeling of control over the new design as it became clear to them that they were responding to the customer, not plugging away blindly at a list of unreasonable management and marketing demands. As a result, the engineers were happier and more effective in their work.

What do you do differently when you manage by empowerment?

STEP ONE: YOU BREAK DOWN ALL ARTIFICIAL BARRIERS.

Do everything you can to prove that you are all part of one group with shared goals. Once you give visibility to the overarching goals of your organization and show employees how they can hook their own aspirations into the company's goals, you'll develop an excited, committed team.

Get to know employees by being around them. Place your office in close proximity to their work space. Scratch the "I'm management and you're not" posture. Deliberately cross the barriers that normally separate managers from workers. Go so far as to spend a week or two working a regular shift in your manufacturing or operations centers. Get some hands-on experience working beside your employees; don't let your lack of experience hold you back.

At Apple Computer, when Jean-Louis Gassee moved from sales and marketing to become the new president of Apple Products, he was open with his employees about the newness of his responsibilities. To be sure he understood what his people at all levels were doing, he worked for two weeks on a manufacturing line, hung out for several weeks with the engineers, and so forth, and in the process gained the fundamental understanding that he needed to lead his huge operation well.

Leading people requires that you stay in touch with them. Because time is scarce, spending it on your employees demonstrates that you respect them and think they're important. At KLA most managers schedule one-on-one meetings with employees every week. This hour is spent talking mostly about key business activities, but inevitably people talk about their interests as parents, athletes, musicians, and volunteers in the community.

When our database specialist, Karen James, completed a rush project in a superb way, I could have given her a spot bonus of several hundred dollars. Instead, because she was in her sixth month of pregnancy, I took her on a shopping spree. It was a surprise. I had her meet me at an unexpected spot, jumped in her car, took out a list of all the nearby baby stores, and we spent two hours buying baby gear. This high-quality time was as much a gift as the things we bought. She is such a valued employee that I wanted to tighten the bond between us before she went on leave. I wanted her to return to work after the baby came. How much more fun it was to go shopping with her than to simply give her a check for $300. And how much better we got to know one another.

Encourage interaction between groups. Jim Kouzes and Barry Posner, in *The Leadership Challenge,* describe a manufacturing manager who admitted she often asked supervisors questions that could not be answered until they talked with their peers. In this way she indirectly forced them to get together.

When Mike Wright took over as Director of Development and Operations for a San Jose division of Critikon, a Johnson & Johnson company, the waste rate was 60 percent and the shipping rate was twenty products a month. The waste rate is now one percent. This group, which hasn't grown appreciably in employee size, now ships 500 to 600 products a month. Mike accomplished this turnaround by transforming a dumpy physical environment into a classy setting to improve morale and setting up the division in an unusual fashion. Instead of dividing people into functional work groups with all of finance together and all of manufacturing together, he placed an accounting clerk next to a buyer, and across the aisle an engineer. In other words, he mixed up groups to break down barriers between departments, keep communications easy, and ensure that people identify with the whole division.

Each year I work with KLA's European managers, who are normally scattered throughout three different countries. In an intensive three-day, off-site meeting, we examine points of conflict that have developed because of responsibility overlays and personality and cultural differences. We let everyone see how well they work together, we tighten relationships between our offices in Germany, France, and the U.K., and we ensure that information gets shared.

Incidentally, valuable information can be passed in two ways. Employees know some things about their work and how the organization runs that you, as manager, will never know unless you ask. When you consult with them and treat them as the valuable resource they are, you gain access to information and insights that can make you and your organization more productive.

STEP TWO: BUILD EMPLOYEES' CONFIDENCE IN THEMSELVES
AND INCREASE YOUR CONFIDENCE IN THEM.

When you are serious about delegating important work, keep the group informed about the budget, staffing, and other resources available for the project. Employees need to know the actual criteria by which their ideas will be judged or they will be likely to propose approaches that are too limited or too extravagant. Then you'll find it easy to criticize and ignore their ideas. On the other hand, if you give them complete information and useful feedback, you are likely to be impressed with the results of their thinking. (If you're not, maybe you hired the wrong people in the first place!)

To build employee confidence, make their jobs as responsible and self-governing as you possibly can. Give them a "client" to be satisfied, a measure of control over how they schedule their work, an identity as an expert in their area, the freedom to talk to anyone in the company to get their job done, and the personal accountability to do their portion of the job right the first time. Relinquish as much control to them as possible.

Will this mean you drop responsibility for what they produce? Not at all—you can't. But you can create a psychological climate to perform well. Take advantage of the new work force's drive to use its talents and capabilities to release you from hour-by-hour supervision of their work. Of course, employees who repeatedly make mistakes and are clearly working beyond their level of competence should be pulled back to jobs that allow them to function well. Realistically, make it clear that you operate under a climate of reciprocity. Having given trust and openness, if you don't get it in return, you will go back to direct supervision. Employees will get the message that everything within the Worth Ethic is mutual in nature. You get what you give. Every time.

Within this climate, the more you trust people to do well, the more reason you will have to continue to trust them. Employees' self-confidence, and your confidence in them as well, will grow with every success.

I was especially touched when Ken Coleman, Senior Vice President of Silicon Graphics, asked me to work with some of the company's long-term employees. Silicon Graphics had grown very rapidly and some early employees were passed over for promotion because of the need to bring in more experienced people to manage the challenges that came with rapid growth. Nothing new here, except for Ken's refusal to watch these early players leave the company, disgruntled and feeling unappreciated. Instead he brought me in to help these people develop their skills, so the next time a promotion was possible they'd be ready.

STEP THREE: LISTEN WITH AN OPEN MIND
AND HIGH SENSITIVITY.

Take the time to sit down with people, use questions to solicit information and stimulate thought, and then pay attention—really pay attention—to the answers. Be sensitive to what someone feels as well as what that person says. These much talked about but too little-used techniques guarantee that a measure of power has truly passed to your employees as they contribute their special insights to the process of identifying and solving work problems.

I can't overstate the importance of learning to listen. You already know that listening to people builds their self-esteem, a kind of honest pride that translates into doing good work. Now I want you to recognize that its value is more than motivational, it provokes ideas that contribute to problem solving. If you use your leadership skills to encourage silent people to talk up and talkers to keep from monopolizing the sessions, you'll have ideas galore. Moreover, the ideas will be practical ones that you can build on and use, provided you are open and share information generously.

Kyle Snyder, KLA's senior technologist, practices what he calls "technical humility" to get innovative products developed in his lab. He is consulted by others in his field, internationally, yet he makes no secret of the fact that he tries to hire people more technically qualified than himself. Then, because he believes in the capabilities of his team and expects them to have ideas that make sense technically, he listens to them, trusts them, and supports them in whatever way possible in their efforts to develop excellent products. Kyle attributes KLA's world leadership in developing complex electronic-imaging inspection systems to a corporate culture of technical humility and the careful listening that results.

I am impressed with the openness of Robert Griffin, Vice President of Human Resources at The Drackett Company, the manufacturer of household brand name cleaners like Windex and Drain-o, in Cincinnati, Ohio. He makes it a point to ask his staff what unmet expectations they have of him, and gets their input on new projects and systems. Then, he listens carefully so that he is clear how he can keep them motivated and happy. It's no wonder that Drackett, of the many Bristol Myers companies, is considered to have the strongest human resources program.

Listening skills can and should be taught. A study by the Center for Creative Leadership in Greensboro, North Carolina, shows that most fired executives are poor communicators. They are loners who mistrust other people, think of discussion as a waste of time, and frequently make insensitive remarks. Personally, I've known many such executives and they are often fine speakers. They couch their own ideas in pungent phrases, but they seem to listen with only half an ear. They concentrate on cutting short the discussion and interrupting to give advice, confident they have the best ideas at hand before anyone else has said a word.

Train people to listen, but also serve as a good role model. Jack Hart is Senior Vice President of Human Resources at Heller International Corporation in Chicago, one of the top financial services companies in the country. Jack is one of the best listeners I've ever met. Years ago I worked for him, and he pried information out of me I didn't even know I had. How? He asked penetrating questions and then sat quietly while I thought and listened while I talked. Jack was especially good at listening to my feelings. He would say things like "It sounds as if you were disappointed about that." Or, "You sound pleased with the program. Why do you think it went so well?" He not only got the information he needed, he taught me to analyze my hunches and to reach useful conclusions.

Good listening isn't passive. It means more than not talking. Ask questions and listen closely to responses. Dig for genuine concerns and conflicts. Pay attention to what people are trying to tell you, even if they don't have well-developed verbal skills. They know things you need to learn.

PHASE THREE: DISTRIBUTE PERSONAL POWER
THROUGHOUT THE COMPANY

Collaborative programs empower employees and help them have input at work. Their success is predicated on cross-fertilizing the ideas of employees—on the manufacturing floor, in shipping, in sales, or anywhere else that they have know-how—with the ideas and insights of middle managers who can communicate and champion proposals to top management.

At KLA, we set up task forces and other collapsible problem-solving teams that involve people from all over the company and from all levels of the company. We give these teams easy access to top management and the authority to negotiate and compromise to reach workable solutions.

Contrast KLA's approach with what happened in several companies where I worked as a consultant. "Quality circles" were set up, with everyone required to participate. The circles worked at first—employees were trained in the formal ways of problem solving, encouraged to say their piece, and helped to write up reports. But managers failed to ensure that the reports were read and that actions, if appropriate, were taken. Employees lost interest and resisted attending meetings that were, in their words, "useless" and "a waste of time."

STEP ONE: MAKE TOP MANAGEMENT'S SUPPORT
HIGHLY VISIBLE.

Without top management's visible support, collaborative programs get saddled with second-class status. There's no one "right way" to empower employees and to encourage participation. A variety of approaches works as long as everyone is involved and everyone knows what is happening. But there's one wrong way to provide collaborative programs, and that's to limit them to lower levels of the company.

Everyone should participate. This means executives, assemblers, secretaries, marketers, shippers, engineers, everyone. Building morale and learning how to problem-solve are nice by-products of collaborative programs, but bottom-line, corporate advantages come from thoughtful cross-fertilization of ideas about how to solve costly problems. For this reason, the program needs to be both universal and visible.

Collaborative efforts have a real impact when middle managers get visible access to top management and top management shares information and implementation authority. If middle managers and executives don't develop an interest in the collaborative programs, workers eventually become disillusioned, because nothing changes. While the collaborative program may meet some of their social needs, it meets no one's achievement needs. Seeing things change as a result of their efforts is what makes people productive. Yet nothing can change if top management holds on to control.

In practice, this means collaborative management cannot be initiated participatively. Top management must make a clear decision to empower employees by setting up a company-wide participative system. Eaton Manufacturing, one of the first large companies to try to install collaboration systematically, did it by formally making participative management a corporate goal and putting its 150 top managers through a three-day training program on collaborative techniques. In this way, the top management team worked participatively itself and modeled the new work style for the rest of the company.

I'll never forget the first time I saw KLA executives in the throes of strong dissension. Several general managers wanted to acquire one company and the remainder of the group was holding back from such a costly commitment. After an intense discussion, a general manager suddenly came up with a third alternative, which was pursuing the top company in the market we wanted to enter. "Wow, that would be like marrying the prettiest girl at the dance," a senior vice president cried, and everyone spontaneously agreed. Like KLA, your company's success at collaboration needs to begin with a visible role model at the top of your company.

STEP TWO: RECRUIT AND TRAIN PEOPLE
TO WORK COLLABORATIVELY.

Even where personal power is clearly distributed and collaboration is successful, such as at Frito-Lay's Kern County plant, it requires special employee selection and training. Turnover at Frito-Lay's plant was 15 percent initially because some recently hired employees just didn't feel comfortable in the open-systems arrangement. Increasingly, companies are using a lengthy set of interviews to ensure that people are not hired unless they are going to perform acceptably and fit into the company's culture. Apple Computer, Hewlett-Packard, and Nordstrom use this approach.

Tom Peters praises the lengthy interview process, noting that the new hire gets the key values of the company instilled through the recruiting process itself. Besides that, if anyone's not going to be comfortable in the company, that person gets ample chance to find it out before accepting a job offer. A lengthy interview procedure gives a job applicant multiple opportunities to meet with various managers within the group that has an opening. Applicants are encouraged to meet with other workers, too, have lunch with them, and get a feel for what's going on and how work gets done in the organization. Flaws, both the applicant's and the company's, are more likely to come to light during a series of interviews than in one interview, however long it goes on.

With a broad training program, the entire recruiting process becomes an opportunity to empower people to be effective. In many companies only managers go to interviewing training. Linda Larsen, the best employment manager I've ever met, insists that anyone who interviews her candidates is trained. Linda emphasizes the importance of training the engineers who conduct the technical screening and the human resources people who review the benefits. She insists that managers and executives, who think they know how to interview because they've been doing it so long, also learn how to plan an interview, how to identify what they should learn, how to ask questions, and how to honestly sell the candidate on the company. People dread interviewing because they resent the time it takes away from work they perceive as more important. Linda helps them understand that their effectiveness is determined by the people hired into the work group.

Collaboration in the interviewing process saves companies the pain of bad hires and prevents the too hasty rejection of someone who might work out well. More than that, it ensures that the candidate is comfortable functioning in a collaborative environment. Once on board, that person should benefit quickly from your training in collaborative skills.

STEP THREE: CREATE A VARIETY OF COLLABORATIVE TEAMS.

Remember that the fundamental goals of collaborative management are two-fold: to make employees feel important, and to use their know-how to make a difference in productivity. You can get people involved, give them personal power, anywhere in the company.

How far can a company go with this concept? W. L. Gore & Associates, manufacturers of Gore-tex fabric and other high-technology products, takes collaboration and personal power further than most companies do today. New employees are often allowed to look for tasks that they want to do, rather than be assigned to jobs that already exist. Employees identify a direction they'd like to follow, form a new team, set objectives, and get to work. Each manufacturing plant is kept deliberately small. Working with just a few hundred people, management can cut down bureaucracy and encourage teams to communicate directly with one another. Pay is set by compensation teams of employee advocates; for additional motivation they also earn stock equivalent to 15 percent of their salary each year. Gore does $150 million in sales annually, has 4,000 employees, and 30 plants worldwide.

At Pontiac's Fiero plant, workers are involved in all levels of decision making. Each worker on the shop floor is part of an operating team that writes its own job descriptions and con-ducts its own inspection and maintenance work. The original one hundred job descriptions have been replaced by only seven. Individual workers take on more jobs and a greater number of duties. And that's not all—they work with the next-level supervisors, discussing production and performance problems and helping to solve them. At the top level, the union shop chairman takes part in the plant manager's staff meetings and knows all the plant's financial data. The plant manager operates on the belief that the combined wisdom and experience of a group is greater than the separate wisdom and experiences of any one member.

When Bethlehem Steel wanted to introduce a $2 million office automation program, it created a task force of office workers and asked them to meet monthly to come up with ways to use the system. One idea was to use the system to improve company-wide communications. The task force rec-ommended that the office automation system provide an elec-tronic newsletter and electronic mail service to move information around the company faster. The company listened, and got what they'd hoped for and more. Reluctant super-visors, who might otherwise have left the equipment to the data entry people, willingly learned its basic features so they could log on to the new communications tool. It's true that the task force spent more time designing uses for the system than top management would have. But by being a part of the pro-cess, the office workers "bought into" the uses they devised.

How do you ensure that team efforts pay off? Choose people who are experts on whatever the team was formed to do. Deliberately select team members from different func-tional areas, because you want the group to develop integrated solutions. Next, be sure they know what you expect them to accomplish and the deadlines they face. Then share power. Give them not just the responsibility, but the resources and authority they'll need to do the job: budget, space, manpower, and time away from regular responsibilities. Finally, review their progress and listen to their problems. You'll get results.

Task forces and committees that operate from principles of collaboration help to ensure acceptance of new ideas and stem people's resistance to change. Human resources managers typically have little organizational power and must operate from their ability to influence and persuade. Consequently, you frequently see them use collaborative teams. For example, when Al Cody, a manager in administrative services at Lockheed Corporation, developed a new mentor program for high-potential managers, he formed a committee of key managers from the company to refine his original ideas. Al gave them the authority to work with general managers to select program participants and to make any changes that would speed up implementation and ensure funding. As a result, he increased the likelihood of the program's success. At Apple Computer, Dorothy Largay, manager of executive development, worked on a similar program to develop key managers. Dorothy formed a committee of Steve MacMahon, employment manager, Debbie Biodilillo, employee relations director, Kevin Sullivan, human resources vice president, and herself. Together they piloted programs of different types, collecting broader data in less time than if Dorothy had worked alone. These are two simple examples of people working together to improve the quality of their work.

The general manager of KLA's newest division, John Schultz, uses the full scope of work teams. The division itself began with engineering development that involved engineers and managers from all over the company. Using resources and solutions they'd already developed in their own divisions on other kinds of products, they brainstormed the feasibility of a complex image-processing product that would require a technological breakthrough. Then, about a year before the design was complete and the product was ready to ship, we had two experienced KLA managers join the team. Richard Long became manufacturing director and Ned Harper became field service manager. We brought a sales manager from outside the company to begin working with the team while two marketing people worked continuously with the engineering group. The involvement of sales, marketing, manufacturing, and field service created constant feedback from the customers to the engineers and ensured a product design that was easy to manufacture and easy to sell.

To generate enthusiasm, energy, and creativity among your employees, you must integrate their practical knowledge and experience into workable solutions to problems. You have to let people see they've made a difference. A significant way to do this is to share the credit for good ideas and the personal power for implementing them. Though you may be reluctant to do either, that's how you develop your employees' Worth Ethic. It's also how to translate their ideas, talents, and skills into productivity gains for you and your company.

STEP FOUR: REWARD COLLABORATIVELY
FOR TEAM EFFORTS.

This is an important step, and a tricky one too. Nearly all compensation systems are based on individual performance. Managers assess employee performance using as many as twenty different criteria, and teamwork is just one of the qualities evaluated. When employees get annual bonuses and pay hikes, they can't see that teamwork cinched their award, if indeed it did. Maybe it was their persistence, or their technical skills, or more likely a combination of skills and talents. If you want to reward someone for outstanding teamwork, for not holding back or trying to snag the glory, you have to reward the team as a team.

A buyer in the purchasing department, for instance, makes a limited contribution to the team's success and may not deserve the same reward as the design engineer on the team. Certainly, the buyer works with the team only in the initial stages of introducing a new product to manufacturing. But without that person's contribution, the team effort would fail. You have to reward every member of the team, collaboratively. If certain employees' performance has earned them special recognition, they can be given an additional bonus.

We developed a special collaborative reward system for the KLA 2020 product development team. The entire team of thirty-five managers, engineers, technicians, and secretaries, plus their spouses, was sent to Hawaii for a week as a reward for meeting their schedule commitments. In this case, we felt the spouses were as much a part of the team as the employees. These people had forgone weekends, baseball games with the kids, Sunday dinners, and evening after evening as their engineering and testing efforts gobbled up all available time. Members of the development team often ate all three meals a day on the job. But in the end they completed the complicated project and delivered it to the customer exactly as promised. If the schedule had slipped somewhat, they still would have received a reward, but a less glamorous one. The team incentive built group commitment and empowered team members to apply performance pressure on peers, as well as to lend a helping hand where needed.

Sometimes you'll find that an outsider, someone not on the team, helps make success possible. When that happens, give a reward for outstanding cooperation to that person. Certainly you want to give spot bonuses and organize events to celebrate team successes, but remember as well those who, for example, arranged the financing or developed the sales graphics. If you can't succeed without them, they need your recognition.

Now that you're aware of the time-saving, idea-generating value of sharing power, you'll no doubt do so in staff meetings, employee committees, team building meetings, task forces, and maybe even formal quality circle programs. As you do, think of your employees as customers. After all, you want to keep them sold on their jobs. A study by the White House Office of Consumer Affairs shows that 96 percent of unhappy customers never complain to the stores where they received poor services or goods, but 91 percent won't buy again from the same place, and, on average, they'll share their bad experience with nine other people.

I think that employees are a lot like customers. They'll tell everyone except you if you treat them shoddily. Treat them well—that is, let them make a difference at work. Give them some control over their workday and the quality of what they do in it, and they'll tell you directly, in their enthusiasm, commitment, and results, that they love their work.

5

A HUNGER
FOR APPROVAL
Recognize the Winner in Everyone

"I bless the world because I bless myself."
—A Course in Miracles

Sue Cummings had worked for a new employment manager, Lynne Forman, only three months before she turned from a solid but uninspired performer into a star. I was curious about the great change until one day I walked into Sue's office just as she was telling Lynne she'd filled another open position. Lynne reached out, squeezed Sue's shoulders and cried, "You did it, you're great, you got another hire!" Later Lynne told me that she opened a bottle of champagne in recognition of Sue's first hire and provided specific recognition of her success two or three times a week. Experiencing this level of warm, personal, and enthusiastic praise, naturally Sue's performance rose. Within six months, the corporate controller was telling a review meeting with the company's CEO and chairman of the board that we should be cloning Sue for our recruiting group.

It's easy to account for this transformation. People want to be winners, not losers. They want to know how they're doing; it's essential to their performance and satisfaction at work.

Approval and recognition are the tools for reinforcing change, and, fortunately for us managers, they are addictive.

Indeed, evidence exists that approval and other affirmations of people's personal worth are actually chemically addictive. In *Fabric of the Mind,* neurosurgeon Richard Bergland says that tears of happiness have a different molecular make-up from tears of sadness. Positive emotions have chemical effects on the body that make people feel good and create a craving for more of these caring responses. As a result of this addiction, people hunger constantly for proof of their own value.

You and I, as managers, most likely count on our families and close friends to make us feel special. But the new work force looks to us for this reassurance. Remember, their support network of family, friends, and community ties is extremely limited. In Silicon Valley companies, nearly half the work force is unmarried, under age thirty, and living far away from parents and childhood friends. And what do we managers know about filling this new role? Do we know how to be friends, express approval lavishly, and build self-esteem in people who are, relatively speaking, practically strangers?

Hardly. We act as if praise and partnership feelings are something frivolous and unnecessary to others. Mostly we take our employees and our families for granted. We squeeze them dry until they have no more help to give, never realizing the resentment we create. We simply expect good work. When we don't get it, we're disappointed, of course, and maybe angry. But when we do get it, we accept it as our due. We give people no special recognition. We continue to assume they are just doing their job and haven't "earned" any special attention.

Admit it. We assume that people know they wouldn't be kept around if they were unqualified and that they know they would be told if they didn't do good work. That should be enough, we think, ignoring what we know about human nature.

The truth is that almost all of us feel a need to come out on top. We need to measure and see how high we've grown. Our self-worth depends on it. So we compare ourselves to others, to convince ourselves we're okay. In a recent psychological study, people were asked to rate themselves on their ability to get along with others. Look what happened: The respondents, selected at random, all rated themselves in the top half of the population. Every single one of them. Fully 25 percent put themselves in the top one percent of the population. This says that, even if statistically speaking most of us are "normal" rather than above average, we all like to think we're special.

We spend a lot of energy trying to prove to others that we are important. We work to increase the size of our offices, our salaries, the number of people we manage, and the number of times and ways we are told we're important each year, month, week, and day. Sure, money counts. Its power makes life a little simpler sometimes. But mostly we just hope that if people treat us as important, we'll finally feel important. We seek the approval of others if only because, when others approve of us, we can begin to approve of ourselves. We're so afraid that we're not special. Perhaps this is why we react so negatively to criticism. It cuts directly to our fear that we're not special and deepens our longing to be worthy of praise.

CRITICISM IS RARELY CONSTRUCTIVE

Dr. Henry H. Goddard, when he was the psychologist at Vineland Training School in New Jersey, measured fatigue in children after criticism and after praise. When they were praised, there was an immediate upsurge of new energy that increased performance. When they were criticized, their energy plummeted.

Researchers studying motivation found that telling a group of adults that they did poorly on solving ten puzzles decreased their performance on a second try. Telling the group it did well, regardless of whether the praise was deserved or undeserved, improved performance on the second try. We probably think otherwise, but "constructive criticism" is almost never constructive.

From my own experience, I know that constant carping doesn't work well. I recognize that it's your prerogative as a manager to assign tasks to your employees and expect them to be completed, but repeated criticism of how employees do their tasks can and often does produce undirected or misdirected activity rather than the results you wanted.

B. F. Skinner, originator of behavioral psychology and the reinforcement theory, warns that while negative reinforcers such as criticism and punishment produce changes in behavior, those changes are often unexpected or even undesirable. In *Tactics*, Edward de Bono says, "The basic problem with punishment is that it leads to resentment and antagonism. It is particularly noticeable in close relationships." The main problem with criticism is that it only identifies what's wrong. It doesn't give specific guidance on how to change or improve. Superficial advice such as, "Work harder," isn't very helpful either.

Real help comes at the experiential level, when a person's good performance is noticed and praised. If a person's performance or attitude absolutely warrants criticism, the person is no doubt aware of his or her poor showing anyway. You will achieve nothing by pointing out missed deadlines or persistent absence from work. Better, then, to skip the criticism and get straight to identifying the problem: "Why has your level of performance gone down?" you might ask. Or, "What's giving you trouble in this area?"

There's a pat formula to keep a person listening to you and invite confidences and clear analysis rather than resentment or anger. It's called an "I" message and has three steps: Describe the behavior without placing blame; state the effect of the behavior in terms of its most concrete results; express your personal feelings about that effect. This is an "I" message: "When your work has typos, I have to reread your drafts several times to catch your meaning. This creates more work for me and irritates me."

"I" messages work because they are the least threatening way to communicate with someone. A "you" message, such as

"You are handing me very sloppy work," is likely to make the listener feel defensive, angry, or discouraged. As a result, the person will begin to make excuses or accusations rather than acknowledge and address the problem. Being logical isn't helpful either, because the most impartial, logical assessment suggests that you think you are smarter, or at least in a position to judge, the other person's actions. "I" messages simply explain to the person the ways in which their actions cause you trouble. They are direct statements to let people know when you have a problem with them. It's up to the listener, then, to decide how to proceed.

APPROVAL PAYS OFF

We know that when people receive approval, recognition, and praise, they become more cooperative and harder working. They not only stick around in the hope of more attention, says a long-term psychological study from the University of Michigan's Survey Research Center, they change and grow in order to win even more approval. We know that when we recognize good performance, we clearly define what we consider to be productive behavior. As a result, our employees can duplicate their good performance easily in the future.

Approval makes people happy just as criticism makes them unhappy. Our employees may know they're doing good work and know we know it, too. Still, saying so promotes their self-worth. Their self-respect soars when they are told, "Your strong presentation got us the Anderson contract. You should do all your reports with desk-top publishing, it looks so professional." Moreover, when the praise is specific, it tells employees what they have to do to get more praise. "You handled Jackson's complaint just the way you should—you listened, were emphatic, and helped provide workable solutions."

We managers know that we should praise the people who work for us. We know praise motivates because we know how it invigorates us. Then why are we so reluctant to use this magic motivator? We can hardly strive for a Worth Ethic if we're stingy with praise. Yet, if we give praise at all, we typically say, "You did great, but next time . . ." That is, we are far more likely to use praise like sandwich bread to surround our constructive criticism and make it palatable than to use praise as the main course.

Saying, "Today I'm going to give out more praise," doesn't usually work. If you try to change by working from the outside, you tend to be very task-oriented and it's tempting to set ourselves goals such as, "Improve morale by praising twice a week." It sounds like an easier place to start because it's tough for most of us to look inside ourselves.

We'd like to ignore our personal reluctance to start passing out approval like poker chips, so many for this employee and so many for that one. Unfortunately, starting on the outside doesn't work. Working from the outside, you'll praise people for a few weeks, then slowly your good intentions will wither and die. Instead, you have to change your internal attitude about praise. You have to nurture yourself. You need to know the value of praise firsthand if you want to use it effectively to promote excellent performance throughout your organization.

BLOCKS TO APPROVAL

What makes us hesitant to pass out praise? Basically, we really can't believe that it's all that important.

YOU HAVEN'T EXPERIENCED APPROVAL MUCH AS INITIATOR OR RECEIVER.

Most of us are unacquainted with approval ourselves and, not knowing its exhilaration firsthand, we discount its potential. This may have begun when we were very small, when no one noticed that we cut up one or two bites of our food successfully. Instead they noticed that we needed help with the rest of it. When we smeared food on our faces, eating ice cream or corn on the cob, someone was sure to notice how messy we were. The same thing happened with neatness. Our parents put their energy into pointing out the messes in our rooms, not the little things we did that were neater than usual.

What our parents didn't realize was that kids pick up table manners with no prodding or criticism whatsoever, provided that the parents practice good table manners themselves. Behavior is a far more powerful instructor than words. Our parents thought all that criticism would make us perform better and be happier adults. But it probably didn't, as Dr. Goddard's research with children indicates. And it definitely didn't make us happy to hear we were always spilling things, not thinking straight, or never doing our chores without being told.

YOU TREAT OTHERS AS YOU TREAT YOURSELF—
WHICH IS PROBABLY CRITICALLY.

We picked up critical habits in our childhood when our parents and teachers felt it was their duty to point out our faults and mistakes, and we internalized them. This means we incorporated our parents' critical approach and now, as adults, talk to ourselves in the same way. I call this self-talk. We mentally tell ourselves that we've messed up, we aren't good enough, and we ought to have done better. We aren't satisfied simply to notice what needs changing and efficiently do it. Instead we worry and we criticize ourselves.

Because we're so hard on ourselves—evaluating ourselves against our ideal view of how we should be or how our parents thought we should be—we're naturally tough on others. We expect them to meet our own high standards of excellence. We take for granted those times they do, but we notice and point out every failure, every slight deviation. We don't understand, any more than our parents and teachers did, that the most powerful instructor is a positive example, and the most powerful single motivator to learning is approval.

YOU ARE UNAWARE.

Long ago we associated approval with love. When we were "good," our parents expressed their love with a word, a smile, a hug, or even something as subtle as eye contact. When we were "bad," they expressed their disapproval. Today, when we don't think we're doing a good job, and our performance doesn't match our internalized high standards of excellence, when we don't think we're as good as we could be and should be, we disapprove of ourselves, abandon our feelings of self-worth, and tell ourselves we're not very good after all.

If this self-flagellation merely made us miserable, it wouldn't matter so much. But the fact is we threaten to destroy our health, cancel our opportunities for personal success, and blast our chances of getting excellent performance from our employees when we habitually look back at past performance flaws and disapprove of ourselves. On the other hand, a considerable body of evidence shows self-approval is good for you.

Self-approval enhances your health. Norman Cousins, in an article for the *New England Journal of Medicine* (and later in his book, *The Anatomy of an Illness*), told how he used positive experiences, such as belly-laughing while watching the "Candid Camera" TV series, to release what he called "hormones of happiness" that brought his body back to health. Like the belly laugh, high praise is a positive experience. Moreover, in the form of self-approval, it can be self-administered. Cousins showed that positive emotions create actual chemical reactions that lead to good health just as stress creates chemical reactions that lead to poor health. (Cousins's article was so enthusiastically received by the readers of this highly respected medical journal that it provoked a greater flood of responses than any other article in the journal's history.)

Self-approval improves your performance. People who concentrate on past failures become less productive as they strive for unnecessary and unrealistic perfection. Andrew M. Meyers and a team of researchers confirmed that less skilled athletes have greater difficulty recovering from mistakes and are more prone to setting high, perfectionist standards. In tests given both to male gymnasts who qualified for the Olympics and their peers who did not qualify, the qualifiers placed little emphasis on past performance failures, while the nonqualifiers worried and sometimes agitated themselves into near panic by mental images of their past mistakes.

Self-approval increases your financial success. People who focus on their self-worth produce stronger financial results than those who primarily target financial objectives. A survey of successful insurance agents by David D. Burns of the University of Pennsylvania turned up a surprising fact: Agents who evaluated their success in terms of their self-worth, job satisfaction, and enjoyment of their work, out-earned agents who evaluated their success entirely in terms of making money, by an average of $15,000.

Because your employees model their behavior after yours, if you focus on self-worth, so will they. They're likely, therefore, to be more productive for you.

PHASE ONE: PRAISE YOURSELF

It's true that we tend to treat others very much as we treat ourselves. If we can't pat ourselves on the back and silently praise ourselves for our own accomplishments, we find it impossible to praise and acknowledge others. So, if you want to develop the praising habit, you must start with feeling good about yourself. When you've succeeded in this realm, you can move out and successfully praise others.

The problem is that most of us have feelings of inadequacy which keep us from feeling praiseworthy. That's not to say we are inadequate. But at some level, often an unconscious one, we feel inadequate because we do not match our vision of ourselves, what we could and should be. It's painful. So painful that we avoid our distress with a common defense mechanism psychologists call projection. We project our own self-critical feelings on others. That way, instead of feeling that we aren't doing a good enough job, we feel that others aren't performing adequately. We become keenly aware of the inadequacies of others as a way to avoid experiencing our own feelings of low self-worth.

I've done this myself. For years, I frequently criticized people on my staff for their tendency to start too many projects at one time. Almost by definition, this meant that projects would be in development too long without being completed. Then, several years ago, I realized that this criticism touched on my greatest drawback as a manager. Out of the dimmest recesses of my memory, I recalled that when my manager in my first corporate position pointed out my tendency to take on too many projects at one time, I responded defensively—a good clue someone has touched on a truth. It took all the intervening years to recognize this was my shortcoming rather than my staff's. I was, in fact, denying I was the source of the problem and had projected on them my tendency to take on too many projects at once.

As a matter of fact, overextending myself is something I've been doing ever since high school. By the end of my senior year I was a leader in two-thirds of the school's activities and on the edge of exhaustion. I was so busy being "somebody," I wasn't having any fun my last year of high school. So I naturally accused my mom of only loving me for what I did and giving me attention only when I was center stage. There was, perhaps, some truth in this, but the real truth was that I didn't think I was valuable unless I was performing and proving my importance to others. I projected my feelings on my mother.

So far, I've talked about "you" in a generic way. Now, I'd like you to get in touch with how you personally feel about praise. If you want to change to the Worth Ethic and work more easily and fruitfully with the new work force, you first need to admit the truth about yourself. I'll help the process along with some self-disclosure that I hope will lead you to examine your own life closely. As you follow me through the CHANGING Process, recall the occurrences that shaped your attitude toward praise, early on, and sort through your own life experiences for those places where you were far better than you gave yourself credit for being.

C CREATE A CONCRETE DESCRIPTION OF THE DESIRED CHANGE.

Are you overly critical of yourself? Frugal with compliments when it comes to acknowledging your accomplishments?

_____

For as long as I can remember, I've been self-critical. I'm dissatisfied when I'm not outstanding in everything I attempt. I'm displeased when I notice that in reality I'm just one more ordinary person. Whatever I achieve in life, I always see ways I could have done better. I wish I could be more accepting toward myself.

_____

H HONESTLY EXAMINE YOUR MOTIVATION TO CHANGE.

How much attention, thought, and time are you willing to devote to this change? How important is it to you?

_____

I've frequently seen my self-dissatisfaction turn up, like an uninvited guest, as dissatisfaction with my daughter, with my own manager at work, or with my friends. My dissatisfaction makes me focus on their flaws instead of enjoying their support and companionship. I resent this critical intrusion, and so do they. I'm better than I was at spotting my projections, but I still feel more dissatisfied than I would like. I want to be happier, and if that means dropping my own dissatisfaction with myself, then I'm all for it.

_____

A   ABANDON THE OLD BEHAVIOR IN YOUR IMAGINATION.

This begins, early in the process, to pull you toward the new behavior you're aiming for. Allow yourself to enjoy life with the change in place. Recall your workday yesterday or the day before. Take note of the everyday things you accomplished. Now glory in them. Allow yourself to feel proud for getting so much done, managing your boss, and being kind to your secretary. Look at all those good, though ordinary things you do each day, and take pride in being such a productive, caring person.

It is very hard for me to imagine being satisfied with myself as I am. I am afraid I will become lazy. But I imagine myself sitting contentedly by the fireplace that blazes in my kitchen, instead of pushing myself to schedule in still one more late-night project. I review my work accomplishments and imagine feeling satisfied that I accomplished most of what I set out to do instead of beating up on myself for the things I didn't get done.

N   NAME THE CHANGE POSITIVELY.

This sort of positive "self-talk" helps you focus on the goal and helps set it in your conscious mind.

Since I wanted to feel that I am enough for me, I said so in my own words, as if it had already happened: "I am satisfied with myself."

G   GIVE ATTENTION TO PAYOFFS.

Payoffs are the good things that result because you rarely praise yourself or others. After all, if some good hadn't come from this trait, you undoubtedly would have dropped it long ago. A common payoff for being bossy and critical of others, for example, is that you're seen as a strong manager, someone who requires excellence in your people. You may be proud of being seen as tough, as someone who is direct and straightforward, who's comfortable "saying it like it is."

The big payoff for being dissatisfied with my own performance is that it pushed me to greater heights. But there was a terrible price attached: Never being truly happy with myself, I couldn't be happy with anyone else, meaning that in any situation there was always more that I wanted from myself and others. My dissatisfaction ensured both high levels of stress and success.

As a result, I was almost afraid to let go of my habit of dissatisfaction with myself and others. I was convinced, after twenty years of consistent adult behavior, that I wouldn't accomplish nearly as much if I allowed myself to be satisfied. On the other hand, being critical of much that my employees, my manager, my family, and my friends did for me kept me unhappy and dissatisfied.

I IMAGINE THE PAST AND SEE HOW YOU BEHAVED.

Look at your past to understand why you behaved as you did. Recall times you accomplished something that should have earned you a significant reward, but somehow didn't. This important step is a chance to gain self-understanding and expand your own awareness of yourself and what makes you tick.

Look very carefully at the behavior of both of your parents, but especially your dad. Research indicates that adults today primarily (though admittedly not always) learned about work and achievement from their fathers.

Look back at the past managers you respected, the people you used as role models and attempted to emulate. Recall eight to ten times over the course of your life when you worked hard on a project and were proud of what you accomplished. Remember what the key person you wanted to impress said to you. If you were lucky, you got a "Good job, Charlie." But chances are this was followed by a "helpful hint" for the future, what parents and managers tend to think of as "constructive criticism." In total, what you heard probably sounded like, "Good job on the Bentley project, Charlie. But next time when you do a proposal, I'd like to see you do . . ."

As you review these events, try to notice the way you generalized or distorted the experience. Look especially for core feelings that became themes, such as, "I'll never be good enough to please Dad," which gets foreshortened to, "I'll never be good enough," or, "Whatever I do, it's never enough." We tend to take several significant experiences—significant to us, anyway—and distort the information a little or a lot and then generalize it.

In my case, I tried to think of experiences that taught me not to recognize and praise my own performance and accomplishments and, as a consequence, not to recognize and praise those of others. I tried to figure out how I acquired the habit of criticizing myself and others and learned to take ordinary, daily achievements for granted.

I recalled working on a tough problem for an advanced algebra class in high school. The instructor told us only one student had solved it in his thirty years of teaching. I worked on the problem nearly every night for three weeks. Then the day before the assignment was due, the teacher mentioned that there were actually two solutions—a long one and a short one.

I'd found the long solution, but all of a sudden my accomplishment wasn't good enough for me. By staying up most of the night, I found the short solution. But when I turned in the assignment, I felt more embarrassed than pleased or proud. My teacher was visibly astounded and said, "Yes, you certainly did find both ways to solve this problem." And that was that!

All through the next week I mentally beat up on myself, saying I shouldn't have shown up the other people in the class, that I'd never have another friend again, and that my teacher and the other students probably thought I was a show-off. Because I operated with a template that said I was "never good enough," I found something to criticize about my performance. Instead of relishing my achievement, I regretted demonstrating my skill.

As I thought back to the algebra experience and other key events in my high school years, I suddenly realized how I'd yearned for public recognition and acceptance. I allowed myself to be a little creative and in my imagination, enjoyed a school assembly held to recognize my solution to the difficult algebra problem. I felt a sort of buzzing, flurrying feeling in my chest when I substituted outright praise and public recognition for the reality of my teacher's noncommittal remark. The locked-up feelings bubbled out as my body responded to the imagined recognition, and I felt exhilarated and proud.

In the wake of that remarkable experience, I imagined a huge family Christmas dinner where my parents talked to my collective aunts and uncles about what a perfect child and diligent student I was. Then I moved forward a few years, in my mind, to my first professional job. I imagined a company meeting at which the president personally presented me with a special award for outstanding innovation. At last I was properly recognized for my role in developing a highly profitable product, which was marketed by the company several years after I left.

In each case, as I let go of the unfortunate memories and mentally experimented with how it might have been, I experienced certain body sensations that naturally would have accompanied the changed experiences. Those sensations became my allies as I gained an understanding of what was occurring within me. I was feeling what it would have been like to receive an abundance of recognition for my accomplishments—and it felt great. I felt so good about all I'd done in the past!

_____

I have hundreds, probably thousands of similar examples, and you do, too. Use this time as a chance to remember some of them.

Relive those old experiences and now pretend that someone treated you the way you want to become. Review each experience you recalled and feel the pride and sense of accomplishment you would have felt if someone had responded to you positively. Resist the temptation to criticize the people who may have wronged you back then. This isn't the time to project your bad feelings or judge their behavior. Instead, gently remind yourself that this is a time to be caring and positive toward yourself, that your goal is to shower yourself with what humanistic psychologist Carl Rogers calls "positive self-regard."

N   NAIL DOWN THE NEW BEHAVIOR
USING MENTAL REHEARSAL.

Imagine the sort of person you'd be today if people had responded differently to you in the past. Fine tune that mental picture of yourself so it matches your goal. Imagine the "new you" functioning in remarkable ways in the future.

This is an important "muscle-building" step. Like developing biceps, setting new habits in place also takes many repetitions. Practice it on five or six different situations. Every day, in real life, practice giving yourself praise and positive feedback. Remember to praise yourself for giving someone else recognition: Catch yourself doing something right. Think of yourself as a champion and you'll become one. Moreover, you'll free yourself to think of your employees as champions, too.

_____

Trying to learn to praise and approve of myself and others, I imagined myself as someone who thinks all sorts of self-supportive and encouraging things and constantly approves of me. I thought ahead to projects that I would be working on and imagined setbacks occurring. Then I imagined telling myself that I'm doing a good job, that I'm patient and capable. I imagined myself overcoming hurdles and I thought about how reliable I was and how I could always be counted on to come through.

G   GRADUATE TO THE NEW BEHAVIOR.

Take every opportunity to model your new behavior for your work group. Tell them how you are using positive self-talk to give yourself approval, and encourage them to do so, too. Let them know it's all right to be positive about their own accomplishments. Ask them questions that give them an opportunity to stroke themselves in an honest, non-egotistical way.

For example, tell them how well you think a particular project is going. Then ask them to explain how they did such a good job organizing it, exactly how they went about it. At appropriate moments, acknowledge their cleverness, even though the actual accomplishments were something the "old you" might have thought ordinary and expected job performance.

I make it a point to have something good to say to at least three people each day, and one of those people has to be my daughter. I try to take the time to ask them questions about their accomplishments and to listen to what they have to say. I want them to know how important their accomplishments are and I want to show them how to stroke themselves.

If you have followed this CHANGING Process along with me, you'll begin to notice a strange phenomenon in the next few months: You'll hear many more positive things about your accomplishments. Most of us receive far more praise and good feedback than we allow ourselves to take in and believe. As you become kinder to yourself, you'll tend to hear the praise that you are now shrugging off. You'll find yourself saying "thank you" more often, because you'll recognize that the compliments you get are well deserved. Once you've changed on the inside, you can move beyond yourself and change your work style and management style.

PHASE TWO: ADD APPROVAL TO YOUR MANAGEMENT STYLE

How do you acknowledge the accomplishments of your work associates, provide them with the recognition they crave, and give yourself the performance payoffs that praise delivers?

STEP ONE: PRAISE PEOPLE IN AS MANY WAYS AS YOU CAN.

Your employees may know that they are doing good work without ever being told. But they won't know that you know unless you say so.

Several years ago, I worked with an executive who, though warm and funny, was notorious for giving only negative feedback to his staff. I counseled Wayne about his problem and, as a result of our talk, he agreed to teach a portion of a performance counseling course on "Giving Positive Feedback." The idea was that he would improve his own awareness and skills by teaching the middle managers who were in the course.

As soon as the session was announced, I began to hear comments in the halls at work. Actually, they were more like mutters, the gist of them being, "What's he know about positive feedback?" Wayne opened the first session with these words: "Everyone," he said, "including me, thinks he can manage people. But so often what we're really engaged in is 'Pimple Management.' We praise by saying, 'Great job, but . . .' and then proceed to point out the pimples." No one complained after that. He won them over with his honesty.

For several days after our initial talk, Wayne had been unwilling to buy into my perspective. So he kept track of the number of times he criticized his people. Once he saw how negative he was, he wanted to change and start over with a clean slate. That's why, on the first day of the training program, he admitted to his negative style of managing. By encouraging the middle managers to laugh with him, a senior executive, he invited them to join him in learning to give positive feedback.

The very people who most crave praise are those we forget most often. Most professionals' jobs have intrinsic value that gives them satisfaction day by day, and visibility at the end of each project. They welcome praise, and respond to it, but they naturally get recognition. On the other hand, the clerks, secretaries, finance, and manufacturing people who accomplish things take a back seat to the R & D engineers who develop new products or the sales people with successes. Nevertheless, the company can't do without these people, and they work just as hard and believe they do as well as anyone else. They don't deserve to be ignored when praise is handed out. In *Thriving on Chaos,* Tom Peters observes that we all believe we regularly go far beyond our job descriptions to get work done. Yet recognition for the outstanding, much less the day-to-day achievements, is markedly absent. Remember, a bit of praise can rev up average performers and turn them into superior performers.

One final word of advice: Avoid creating suspicion in your employees. You don't want them to interpret your actions as manipulative, so share straightforwardly your intentions and goals to praise more. Trust them to welcome your openness as well as your approval. Trust them to understand your sincere desire to be more approving toward yourself and toward them.

Trust is, after all, the biggest compliment any one person can give another.

STEP TWO: RECOGNIZE PEOPLE IN WAYS THAT ARE
INDIVIDUALLY MEANINGFUL.

No one expects you to develop a separate recognition plan for each employee, yet it's unreasonable to treat everyone equally. In matters of recognition and reward, everyone is likely to want and need something different.

To make praise effective, praise different people differently. For example, recognize that you are talking to a person who appreciates fast results when he telephones you to ask for a piece of equipment and assures you he's already researched costs and found the best deal available. Obviously, then, your immediate review of the cost comparisons and a short, thoughtful discussion of his recommendation shows support. Go to the next step and specifically praise his thoroughness and promptness as a part of giving the go-ahead. Your response will be the kind of praise he'll talk about for months to come.

If you have a flamboyant vice president of sales who generates fantastic sales figures, you might duplicate the idea of ETC Carpet Mills Ltd., a carpet manufacturer in Santa Ana, California, and hold a "coronation" party for your "Prince of Sales." Flamboyant people aren't embarrassed by extravagant praise. They thrive on it.

As for the faithful who work day after day, or night after night, doing what's expected of them without fanfare, I recommend the unexpected gesture. The city of Fort Wayne, Indiana, declared a "Snow Day" late one summer afternoon and had a party. City employees were treated to an ice cream buffet and the personal thanks of their director.

Francis Loeb, managing director of Loeb AG, a Swiss department store chain, does the unexpected, too. He often drops by Saturdays and at the end of the night shifts to say good night to the workers who have taken the less convenient shifts. The Department of General Services for the City of New York awards employees who use less than a day of sick leave a year with an afternoon off to see a major new motion picture. The $1,600 cost in 1985 far outweighed the saved sick leave expense, $250,000. And who can put a price on the pleasure of being paid to play hooky to see a movie?

Your most meaningful kind of recognition may be completely off target to someone else. Years ago, when I worked in Saigon, a Vietnamese driver drove several of us to work each morning. This driver was reticent and a bit sulky. On more than one occasion I saw him figure out how to avoid doing extra work for people he regularly transported to the office. Yet he showed me special courtesies. He took me places to pick up reports. He carried documents to sites all the way across the city for me. Why? I think, first of all, because I learned his name and used it. I learned something about his family and the village he came from. To me, he wasn't one more nameless Vietnamese. He was another human being, one I cared about and someone who regularly made my work easier and smoother. I voiced my appreciation for the way he scooted through Saigon's traffic jams, and he reciprocated by being reliable and kind. Before I left Saigon, he showed his appreciation by offering to drive me and a friend through intermittent enemy fire to a historic Cao Dai temple I was eager to see. All because I took the trouble to notice him.

Frequent nagging by my co-workers hadn't improved the driver's attitude. Logically, an itemized account of errors might seem to help a person identify problems, but it doesn't address the need to motivate a person to change. Besides, people usually know what they're doing wrong. So, while pointing out a person's faults may feel good to you, it's unnecessary. What's needed, pragmatically, is a re-ordering of priorities.

There is some truth to the old joke, "How many psychologists does it take to change a light bulb? . . . Just one, but he really has to want to change."

Change is internally motivated. The higher an employee's self-worth, the more likely he or she will want to change and develop to full potential. Praise opens the door to self-esteem and thus to growth. If my driver in Saigon had been reckless, what could I have done? Scream, of course, then praise him lavishly for whatever I honestly found praiseworthy.

This approach may seem overly idealistic to you. Admittedly, there are situations that demand simple directions and immediate responses. It's reasonable to tell a typist to correct a typo on a letter going out in the afternoon mail. A reminder or directive is a very handy Band-Aid. It's just not a cure for poor performance.

STEP THREE: GIVE SPECIFIC PRAISE.

To keep praise fresh and motivating, don't let it become routine. Saying, "Nice job, folks," every Friday afternoon at four o'clock isn't praise, it's habit, much like giving your spouse a good-bye kiss each morning before you leave for work. It may be a nice routine, but it doesn't convey enough information to guide future behavior.

Here's how to make praise special: Smile at, look at, and speak directly to the person, use the person's name, then say exactly what the person did to earn your esteem. Saying, "Good work," won't suffice. The words, "You're terrific, because you found out what the customer wanted, figured out how to adapt our product effectively, and contributed to reaching our sales target this quarter," make an employee's feet point in the right direction again for the next quarter.

Brief praise is better than none at all, but specific praise accompanied by at least a short explanation of impact is best. Once, as an experiment in a training program on performance coaching, I asked each person to stand and deliver a bit of praise to someone else in the room. Some people really had trouble receiving that praise. They did a lot of different things to deflect the praise, such as saying, "Yes, but . . ." We talked about the difficulty people have accepting praise, and here's what one middle manager said amidst sounds of agreement from virtually everyone in the room: "I was embarrassed because what I was being praised for simply wasn't that big a deal to me. I loved hearing it, but it was actually just part of my job."

We're all skillful at discounting the praise we receive. I once approached Brad Long, then the head of my work group, and told him I thought he was a truly outstanding presenter and that I wanted to learn from him. I asked, very sincerely, if he would tell me how he developed this skill. At first, Brad treated my request as a joke. When I said I truly wanted to learn from him, he said, "Come on, Kate, I know you're trying to set me up. Just tell me what it is you want." He insisted he was an average presenter, though in reality he was an extremely skillful speaker. As I got to know him over the years, I realized he found it impossible to accept personal praise beyond a basic, "Good job, Brad." But that doesn't mean he didn't like hearing praise.

STEP FOUR: LISTEN TO EMPLOYEES DAILY.

I hope you ask yourself each day, "What can I do to make my employees feel better about themselves and their work?" I know that, on occasion, you revise their job content or do something tangible such as hand out certificates and awards as a means of positive reinforcement. Still, the simplest and most powerful form of acknowledgment is to listen. Giving someone the gift of your full attention is a very strong way to affirm a person's value to you and to show you appreciate their ideas. Andy Grove, CEO of Intel, talks about the value of one-on-one meetings in his book *High Output Management*. At KLA, managers give one-on-one time to all direct reports, usually weekly and typically for an hour, with agendas set by the employees to cover ideas and problems that are important to them. This reaffirms our belief that employees are worth listening to.

Practice turning your attention to others by asking what you can do to help them, then listen to their answers. Listen thoughtfully, to understand both the content and intent of what they say. While you listen, simultaneously try to keep in mind the speaker's unique context, their background and experience as you know it, so that you hear what the person has to say without confusing it with your own point of view. Don't distract yourself with thoughts about what you're going to say next. Concentrate on giving the rare gift of total concentration to the speaker. Listen so that when you do speak, you address both the content and the feelings of that person.

Most of us are far more skilled in dealing with content and logic than with emotions. Consequently, we tend to ignore our employees' feelings. Both are important. For example, I once gave an employee an outstanding performance review, only to hear her discount my recognition of what she had done. To be sure, I responded to her words by telling her even more specifically how well she had done and what her contributions meant to me personally and to the group's overall success. But I also responded to her by pointing out that I sensed she was having trouble accepting my praise. I asked her to tell me what she was experiencing inside, and she said she couldn't believe she was really that good. Finally, as the realization soaked in, she began to beam. Because I had listened and helped her expand her self-worth, her performance over the next months continued to soar and constantly surpassed my expectations.

Here's an experiment you might try to test the tremendous affirming power of listening and paying attention to feelings. At the end of your next heated discussion with someone, say, "You're right." Don't say it sarcastically or in a defeated manner. Then wait for a dramatic decompression in the atmosphere. There's no faster way to affirm someone's worth. It means you not only listened, you agreed!

STEP FIVE: PRACTICE EXPRESSING YOUR APPRECIATION.

The final step in learning to praise others is to practice. Practice a lot. Set yourself daily and weekly goals. No one will complain. It's not as if you were practicing on the tuba. Or haven't you noticed that people rarely tire of praise?

Ken Blanchard, author of *The One-Minute Manager*, talks about one-minute "praisings" and their positive influence on the work environment. Blanchard recommends setting aside two one-hour blocks of time each week just to praise employees by "catching someone doing something right." Commend people in front of others and you give them a chance to enjoy the glory doubly. You also draw the attention of anyone within earshot to what you consider praiseworthy.

Managers manage differently, once they overcome their objections to praising people's good work. You will, too. You can't spend part of every day looking for good results to praise and have low self-worth. Looking for the positive in people keeps you looking for the positive in yourself. Increasingly, you'll feel better about yourself, respectful of others' contributions, more generous with your time, more positive and productive. When any one of us feels good about ourselves, when our self-worth is high, we perform better. That's a documented fact supported by numerous research studies. You'll also find yourself looking for ways to change your company so that other managers, work groups, and departments have the opportunity to see the power that resides in simple praise and recognition.

PHASE THREE: INTRODUCE COMPANY-WIDE RECOGNITION SYSTEMS

What can one manager do? You can do what you can on your own. Keep careful statistics on improved productivity and effectiveness, so you can prove recognition works. Support those who have the power to make other changes. Here are two places to begin.

STEP ONE: INSTALL COMPANY-WIDE SYSTEMS THAT BROADCAST ACCOMPLISHMENTS.

Excellent companies organize and systematize to reinforce winning. The fundamental criterion for doing so is this:

Does the current system elevate employee self-worth? Does it make employees feel like winners? Does it tell them that you love the work they do for you?

People who get things done need to be recognized company-wide, and there are scores of ways to do this. "Thank you's" posted on bulletin boards, letters to their managers, dinner awards, articles in newsletters, "Idea of the Month" awards, photographs in a "Hall of Fame" in employees' buildings, and plaques presented to work groups are all effective.

It costs next to nothing to broadcast that you believe certain employees are outstanding performers. Recognition of this sort costs the company only the time and commitment to plan for recognition opportunities and the effort it takes to notice employees' contributions. It's worth the effort. Whenever a company pays attention to a certain behavior, it tells people that the behavior is important, promotes more of that kind of behavior, and boosts the morale of the recipient. The new work force needs to feel worthy and it wants that feeling externally confirmed.

There's no one best way to praise because each organization has its own charter of things to get done, each group has its own idea of what's meaningful, and each person responds differently to various methods of recognition. Try anything, then stick with what your people respond to with the most enthusiasm. To some, however, a paper chit is a childish game, to some boasting about themselves is rude, to some parties are out of place in the work world. Yet each of these ways of recognizing praiseworthy efforts is working successfully right now in places where it is meaningful to the people involved.

At Silicon Graphics in Mountain View, California, Ed Nelson, Vice President of Operations, uses a bulletin board recognition program. When a product is packed, every test technician or quality inspector signs a customer response card inviting customers to send in their comments. Many customers do just that, and most of what they say is complimentary. Up go the cards and employee morale.

In Walnut Creek, California, the police chief gives out

"champion cards" to anyone on the force who goes out of the way to help another policeman on the street or inside the department. This emphasizes positive action and counteracts the negative aspect of a policeman's basic duty: catching someone doing something wrong.

Every issue of Delta Airlines' employee publication sets the tone for all managers by listing employees who have proved particularly compassionate toward passengers in need of help. The process of identifying such actions is well known to all employees.

At KLA, we have all-employee quarterly meetings at which our president talks about the company's performance and presents awards. Engineers who submit a patent request or document a proprietary technical development receive awards. We also recognize employees who have made recommendations that were used in our Profit Improvement Program.

At Transco Energy in Houston, president George Slocum holds quarterly "bragging sessions" to let people boast a bit. Slocum expects to save $18 million over the next two years simply because departments want to be recognized at these meetings for their cost-cutting schemes.

Ken Coleman, Senior Vice President of Silicon Graphics in Mountain View, California, started an annual contest to recognize the people who stand for "The Best Spirit of the Company" in the opinion of the majority of employees. Ken sends this group of twelve to Hawaii as a reward, accompanied by Vice President of Human Resources, Jennifer Konecny. Together, they brainstorm ways to drive their values throughout the company. This is important because 40 percent of the 1,500 employees have been with the company for less than a year, and such rapid growth threatens to devour Silicon Graphics' core values.

These public recognition programs create a great many opportunities to recognize employees. Volume is important. Companies with a prestigious president's award, given to only a couple of people each year, invariably upset more people than they award. It's impossible to single out two or three people without leaving many people wondering why they weren't included. They're likely to reason: "I just wasn't in tight with the right people." To avoid having employees reach such conclusions, make sure they know exactly how people were selected for recognition. That means the criteria have to be clear enough to write down, and a significant number of people have to be recognized each year. After all, you do have a lot of above-average performers, don't you? As a guideline, IBM strives to recognize in some public way 40 percent of its 40,000 employees each year. Surely you and I can do as well.

STEP TWO: PAY FOR ACHIEVEMENT.

Use money as a reward, too. If you don't, your employees will get the distinct idea that you don't really mean what you say. Money is a powerful recognition tool, provided you pay for the kind of performance you want to see repeated again and again. Use your compensation options to say, "Great job—and thanks."

As a manager, you may not feel you control how your company dispenses money. Yet you have at your discretion a very powerful tool—paid time off. I'll never forget my pleasure and surprise when, after just six months in a new job, Jack Hart, then the vice president of human resources at Impell, gave me a couple of days off, with pay. I'd just spent two weeks of extremely long days, providing training to managers in our other regional offices. The days off were a special reward, his way of saying thanks for a good job. Jack got a lot of mileage out of those two days he gave me. I learned that a period of intense work would earn me a short breathing spell to take care of myself and my family. It tightened my commitment to perform my very best in every situation, no matter what the immediate personal cost, because I knew I would be recognized and appreciated.

Recognizing outstanding performance by paying for it is an especially powerful motivator if the money closely follows the performance, and if it's clear that the money is a reward for some specific feat. Typically, companies believe they're "paying for performance" because they attempt to tie annual merit increases to a person's performance over the course of a year. In actuality, the difference between the percentage increase of the outstanding performers and average performers is probably only 3 to 4 percent. Also merit increases are scarcely timely since they are tied to annual review dates rather than specific performance accomplishments.

For this reason, at KLA we've created a "spot bonus" pool. So long as the groups stay within their budget, the managers of the divisions can give out this money however they choose. A manager may vary the form the bonuses take. They may come as actual money, paid days off from work, or a weekend away for the employee and spouse. The idea is that spot bonuses follow key accomplishments immediately and take a form that's meaningful to the employee.

Here's an ingenious reward program: Early in 1987, president Jerry Saunders of Advanced Micro Devices in Sunnyvale, California, created a cash awards program to reward top performing employees and take the sting out of nine quarters of recession. In colorful comic book format, he announced six $1,000 prizes each month for "Dragonslayers"—employees making extraordinary efforts to overcome exceptional obstacles and satisfy customers; four $500 prizes for "Dragonbusters"— employees making exceptional efforts to eliminate problems between the company and its customers; and a year-end drawing for a trip to England, home of St. George the Dragonslayer.

Recognition energizes us managers to work harder and better, and it can do the same for our employees once we get comfortable with recognizing people honestly and frequently. Remember, as members of the new work force, our employees may have little opportunity to be recognized outside the workplace. It's up to us to fill the role of company as family.

As managers, once we learn to be positive about our own accomplishments, we can approve, recognize, and positively reinforce employees' achievements personally in our daily interactions with them. The company can broadcast their accomplishments and pay for performance, too. Our approval and recognition build employees' self-worth, cooperation, and all other aspects of the Worth Ethic in our organization, so people feel like winners and work like winners. Naturally, the company wins, too.

6

THE INTUITION-INNOVATION LINK

Amazing Truth about Creative Managers

"My understanding of the fundamental laws of the universe did not come out of the rational mind."
—ALBERT EINSTEIN

In 1980, I conducted a program in creative problem solving for a group of managers. I'd run dozens of these programs before. In this class, for the first time, one person had a perfect score. He had solved a nearly impossible problem on his own. Naturally, I was eager to see what the group did with his unusual but correct solution.

To my amazement, no one listened to him. He tried several times, unsuccessfully, to help the group see another way to approach the problem, and then gave up. His solutions didn't fit their perspective, and he didn't stick by his beliefs. He tried, then withdrew from the group. As a result, the group score was less than half correct.

That group of managers had someone in their midst who could have guided them to a perfect solution if the innovator had pushed harder or the rest of the group had paid attention to him. That day they learned their first important lessons about using creativity and nurturing it in others: Be open and be persistent.

BE OPEN.

We know that employees need to use their capabilities to the fullest in order to find satisfaction in their work. And no doubt you recognize the need for their creativity somewhere within your company. However, if the R & D lab and marketing department are far removed from your daily responsibilities, you may not see a direct need for developing your own intuitive skills or supporting creativity in your particular group. You may feel your work tasks are too ordinary to demand something as exotic as creativity. You may shy away from dealing with creative people, thinking they're unnecessary or cause too much trouble.

Creativity can illuminate a problem anywhere a person is allowed to have an impact. Even in your group. Tom Peters points out that most improvements come from creating committed champions out of ordinary employees. Your employees need to see their best ideas translated into high productivity and useful results. Moreover, to put their ideas to work, they need you, managing flexibly and supporting them by using your intuition to smooth the work path. When you let employees have that creative impact, you stimulate incredible involvement and enthusiasm.

For all these reasons, companies look for practical creativity. Ninety percent of the nearly 1,000 executives surveyed by Arthur D. Little in 1985 said they had a growing need for innovation in their companies. Moreover, 75 percent of the executives said they felt that special skills and knowledge were required to manage the innovation process well. That observation is loaded with implications for those of us who wish to promote the Worth Ethic of the new work force.

BE PERSISTENT.

While innovation frequently begins with what management guru Peter Drucker calls a "monomaniac with a vision," good ideas remain just that until Drucker's law is applied:

"Everything must degenerate into work if anything is to happen." Thomas Edison succeeded in inventing the light bulb only after several thousand failed attempts. When my mother pointed to her tray of Christmas cookies and said, "They're a labor of love," she meant she'd created them with pride, sacrifice, and a mess in the kitchen that went far beyond the ordinary. Innovation thrives where people invest energy and time to move from new knowledge and inspired intuition to a final, practical product.

If you don't push your own ideas, who else will? When a researcher at a major oil company invented a pesticide but allowed his discovery to lie buried on page 25 of his report, his formula went unnoticed. Five years later, the company had to reinvent the product.

Rosabeth Moss Kanter, in the *Harvard Business Review*, reports that 165 middle managers from different companies who effectively managed highly innovative projects had the same comfort with uncertainty and change and the same inclination to work hard and persevere until they succeeded as did the R & D scientists at the Center for Creative Leadership in Greensboro, North Carolina. That's not all. These same middle managers were long on tact and insight into the politics of their organization. They had a clear sense of who they could depend on when critical decisions were about to be made. In the management arena, innovation isn't mysterious. It's a matter of gut instinct, practical action, and persistency.

Decline to push your good ideas, and both you and your company lose out. I was hired at Impell Corporation by Gary Berger, in 1981, to develop training programs. His manager, the vice president of human resources, wanted us to begin with a program on performance evaluations. I felt, however, after meeting with managers from all over the company, that we could have more impact working on sales training first. Berger hesitated to cross wills with his boss unnecessarily. I, on the other hand, for one of only three times in my career, persisted with my line of reasoning even though the discussion deteriorated into an argument.

I'm grateful to Berger for not labeling my behavior as insubordination and, ultimately, for compromising. We began two performance evaluation programs immediately and then, within three months, started the sales training program. The results were dramatic in terms of our careers. Berger expanded his responsibility and the company's services, eventually selling technical training programs to Impell customers. As for me, my broad exposure to managers landed me a generalist position in the largest division. The training paid off for the company, too: Sales calls increased by nearly 40 percent the year following the training.

CREATIVITY PAYS OFF

Thinking intuitively is a profitable endeavor. Change is inevitable in today's competitive business environment, but change in itself doesn't guarantee improvement. Yet, creative managers with a practical bent have established an excellent record for generating profits and renewing organizations.

In a test at Newark College of Engineering, eleven of twelve company presidents who had doubled sales in the previous four years scored unusually high in precognition (intuition). Somehow, these company presidents knew things in advance of their occurrence, and they put that knowledge to work to increase their corporate sales. A control group of presidents with average sales records showed no such special talents. After studying over 2,000 managers, Weston Agor, author of *Intuitive Management*, reports many executives readily admit to relying on intuition to make some of their most successful decisions. Research by Douglas Dean and John Mihalasky, reported in their book *Executive ESP*, also shows a positive correlation between a CEO's performance, his intuition, and a high profit record.

I've seen intuition pay off in KLA's strategic and product decisions, too. In February 1985, I provided a presentation at an off-site management meeting that addressed possible actions in the event of a semiconductor downturn. I was nearly hissed off stage because the managers present could not see a serious problem coming. Even the top management team admitted they had only a "feeling" we should get prepared. Yet, over the next six months, we implemented three of the six steps we'd agreed on. As a result KLA was one of the few companies in the semiconductor business that remained profitable during the industry's worst downturn. I'm inclined to believe, as a result of this and similar experiences, that intuition is another form of logical thinking—one in which the steps of the process are hidden in the subconscious. Paul Cook, founder and Chairman of the Board of Raychem Corporation, was asked whether he used much intuition in his decision making. Cook replied that nearly all of his decisions were based on intuition, and that the only major decisions he regrets were ones not based on it.

On occasion I've ignored my own intuitive feelings with unfortunate results. I once hired a manager, even though my intuition kept nagging me to say no. I'd interviewed dozens of people before he came along, and he seemed ideal. I told myself my intuition was wrong until, after a year, his performance was going up and down so much that we mutually agreed he would be better off in a different work environment. Only later did I learn that a problem with cocaine lay beneath his work performance problems.

The development of intuition, or gut instinct, is so important in business that companies encourage it. Over half the *Fortune* 500 companies support training in creative thinking and problem-solving to gain a competitive edge. At Stanford University, MBA students are now offered a course called "Creativity in Business." Michael Ray, the principal professor, introduces his numbers-oriented students to the benefits of Zen meditation, Hindu chants, the I Ching, and various altered states of consciousness. Ray believes that exposure to these alternative philosophies will help them be more resourceful and intuitive in finding solutions to business problems and implementing those solutions effectively.

At 3M Corporation, the company's 6,000 scientists are paid to spend up to 15 percent of the time on their own ideas. Their projects are supported by their own Senate and Technical Forum.

General Foods' Toronto office created an Idea Center, a big room with a sweeping view of hills, trees, and sky. There are big chairs, interesting sculpture, a stereo system—all to help occupants do some unrestricted and non-linear thinking about their projects and problems. The room became so popular for meetings, General Foods built more like it to keep up with the demand for its use.

Peter Ueberroth headed up the 1984 Olympics and generated a $250 million surplus in the process by using the creative thinking skills taught him by management consultant Edward de Bono. General Electric developed self-diagnostic dishwashers by using the brainstorming techniques taught by Synetics of Cambridge, Massachusetts.

Psychologist Arthur Reber of Brooklyn College found that people who use intuition have a genuine competitive edge over those who consciously try to think their way through a product innovation process or other exceptionally subtle task. By stimulating creative approaches to business, companies get the results they're after. In addition, employees enjoy the respect of others and the sense of personal worth that come with using their creative potential.

BLOCKS TO CREATIVITY

Acknowledge the value of practical creativity on the job just once, and you'll want to foster it in yourself and your employees. Some younger employees, raised in the Worth Ethic, await your invitation to fire up their creative talents. But unfortunately life dampens the creativity and imagination of most of us long before we reach the office. So we probably need to unleash our creative fires.

As students, we are taught to come up with the "right"

answers and not to question our teachers. Stan Gryskiewicz at the Center for Creative Leadership reports that creativity test scores normally drop sharply once children enter school, followed by a steady decline as their "education" progresses. Naturally, if we develop in an uncreative environment, we grow into adults who don't feel comfortable with the notions of innovation, intuition, and creativity. This doesn't mean you and your employees are without creative talents. It means you aren't using them.

Let's look at the five primary obstacles to creativity as conceived by James Adams in *Conceptual Blockbusters* and David Campbell in *Take the Road to Creativity and Get Off Your Dead End.* You may recognize your own block in the list. Gain insight into your own feelings and you can help your employees as well.

ARE YOU AFRAID OF FAILURE?

Most of us have grown up to feel we should be rewarded when we produce the "right" answer and punished when we make a mistake. When we fail, we are made to realize that we have let others down, usually someone we love. Similarly, we are taught to live safely. We think over every idea carefully because we can't risk failure. We know that anything new and untried is likely to fail, at least in its initial version. Consequently we form committees. We appoint teams. We avoid risk whenever possible.

As a young person, did you ever spend a disastrous day making cookies and burning them, or building a model plane and ruining it, then have a parent complain about the mess before recognizing your good efforts? No wonder we're uncomfortable with innovation. We aren't trained to tolerate mistakes, our own or others'. As children, if our failures were mostly overlooked or, better yet, considered part of the learning process, then as adults we're likely to keep on trying to innovate.

When my daughter Catherine was two and a half, she stunned me by demonstrating eight different ways to get in the bath tub: frontwards, backwards, across the toilet, standing on the tub rim, and so forth. Of course, water was everywhere. She'd been in and out of the tub at least two dozen times during her experimentation. I might have punished her for the mess and perhaps she would have still turned out creative (as she is, anyway). Instead I praised her, told the story in front of her many times, and in a number of ways enjoyed this new expression of her selfhood. As a teenager she is remarkably creative and a good problem solver. I even run some of my work dilemmas past her and find her advice remarkably perceptive.

Maybe you think I should have lectured my daughter on the dangers of slipping in a wet tub. I don't believe she was in any real danger. She was, after all, joyously slipping and sliding around, totally relaxed, and I was nearby at all times. However, I'll admit that reasonable caution is always sensible and quite different from fear of failure. If you have an idea for building a better lap-top computer or perfecting an artificial intelligence software package for machine shops, you'd be acting reasonably cautiously if you held on to your present job until you'd developed a business plan, hired a management team, and obtained the backing of a venture capitalist. There is, indeed, a huge gap between being rash and being a risk-taker. Wise risk-takers pin down the risks and then decide whether or not they're ready to proceed and willing to suffer the consequences of possible failure.

Adams suggests, in *Conceptual Blockbusting*, that when you can't decide whether to push a creative idea or not, you should develop a catastrophic expectations report. He recommends that you consider what would happen if everything went wrong in your plan. In the process of analyzing worst-case possibilities, you substitute your analytical capability for your fear of failure.

ARE YOU OBSESSED WITH ORDERLINESS?

Now and then we all suffer from a touch of insecurity and wish everything could be safe, secure, and orderly. We tend to think, then, that the old ways of doing things were after all the best. Unfortunately, well-refined products and methods of manufacturing, marketing, and managing have a way of becoming outmoded and outdated. The time comes when you must, say, streamline a manufacturing process and that means experimenting and putting up with some disarray until you can sort out various ideas. Your ultimate goal is to develop an orderly manufacturing line, of course, but getting there may be anything but orderly.

Here's another example. Early in my career I met a communications consultant who refused to introduce video taping into his presentation skills workshop. His old approach had paid him quite well for years, so he saw no reason not to reproduce it. His excessive respect for what he had established kept him from improving his workshop by using this tremendous new technology.

Perhaps like a lot of us, he heard his parents tell him once too often to tuck his shirt in, straighten his room, and make a decision and stick with it. I don't know for certain. I do know an obsession with orderliness is rooted somewhere in the past. Whether it shows up in the guise of absolutely refusing to change "what is," feeling uncomfortable with ambiguity, or simply delaying change to avoid confusion, it makes us more rigid than reasonable and more comfortable than successful.

Recently I completed a program with Fred Jacob, newly promoted Vice President of Operations for a consumer products company. Formerly director of manufacturing, Fred had assumed responsibility for R & D and engineering as well. His most important new responsibility was to work closely with the vice president of marketing to develop broad new product categories for the company. Unfortunately, he never seemed to have the time to get involved in this new assignment. In reality, he felt so comfortable managing the day-to-day work of his organization, he was reluctant to invite the chaos of the new, unstructured projects into his workday. Once he acknowledged and faced that fear, he found the needed time and soon abandoned the day-to-day responsibilities in favor of his new challenges.

ARE YOU INCLINED TO JUDGE TOO SOON?

If you're unwilling to tolerate ambiguity and general disarray, you'll soon bump up against the most irresistible block of all—judging ideas too quickly. People who select the right way very early in the decision process and quickly say, "Let's get on with it," pride themselves on saving time and avoiding confusion. That's not all bad, particularly if the decisions require straightforward analysis and impartial judgment. In such cases, as soon as the right or wise answer is reached, it's time to move ahead on implementation. As a matter of fact, it's good management practice.

Suppose, however, that you face a problem with more than one answer or you face a problem unlike any you've faced before. If you exercise your judgment too early, you may reject an imperfect idea that could have been refined. You may kill off an idea that could have led, through a brainstorming or integration process, to a far better idea. By tolerating a bit of ambiguity, you increase your chance of developing a better idea in the end. Still, it's worrisome to hold off making a decision.

Judging begins early in life, when most of our parents communicated clearly that there was a right and a wrong way to do everything. In my own case, I crashed head on into this attitude every Sunday after our family dinner. My job was to do the dishes, and each week I was eager to try out some different way of washing them—sometimes moving dishes from the left, other times moving the dishes from the right, sometimes doing all the dishes at once, other times washing and letting one batch drain, while I wiped off the counter, and so forth. But my mother, from years of experience, knew already that many of my ideas were not improvements. Instead of letting me experiment, she wanted me to do it her way. Because I was more of a rebel than an accommodator, we argued.

On this particular issue of dishwashing, I never gave up. Years later, I came to appreciate these childhood conflicts because they taught me that I could safely persevere in my beliefs. But many children, knuckling under to forcefully given directions and punished for disrespect, grow up to be adults who expect to be told what to do and how to do it. As a result, they accept the constricting demands of managers who assume that they know best and expect to be followed mindlessly. In the process, they lend inadvertent support to managers who judge too early. Moreover, they form the habit of giving in rather than standing up for their own good ideas. If your employees are as unwilling to push their ideas as you are overly anxious to judge and arrive at an immediate answer, you'll conspire to block innovation.

ARE YOU UNABLE TO INCUBATE YOUR IDEAS?

This block to creativity is second cousin to being too quick to judge. The result's the same, a decision that's timely rather than outstanding. The cause is rooted in poor planning that doesn't provide time for the original ideas to incubate and hatch a better solution, plus a general wariness of the unconscious mind's ability to produce anything better than the conscious mind can produce. Many achievement-oriented managers are reluctant to rely on intuitive thinking.

In college, most of us had the experience of studying something the night before a test, a list of math formulas or French verbs, for example, to awake and find we knew them "cold." You've probably gone to bed worrying about a problem on at least one occasion and had the solution pop into mind the next morning. Perhaps you've come up with a soothing phrase or two that averted a serious argument. I've found that when I prepare for a meeting well ahead, my unconscious mind often comes up with an unusual approach or original idea before the time of the meeting.

If these examples sound familiar to you, you've experienced the unconscious mind at work. Regrettably, most of us are under too much time pressure to use the incubation process effectively. I like to proceed with daily tasks while my unconscious goes to work mixing and matching even the craziest ideas into a unique and valuable solution. Where decisions are acted on precipitously, the results of incubation can be integrated later, but at what a costly and avoidable consequence!

ARE YOU UNWILLING TO BE PUSHY?

It's easy to see how this block develops. Not only do parents stomp on our creative attempts at home, particularly if they're loud or messy, but teachers and the school system in general ridicule us if we don't conform. We're trained to give the usual answer to questions on tests, arrive at physical education classes in the approved, standard gym suit, and attend with regularity even the most poorly organized classes taught by inept teachers. Research of school systems shows that teachers tend to select conformers as their "pets," and ascribe irritating and naughty traits to the creative child who asks daunting, difficult questions.

ARE YOU USING THE RIGHT ROLE AT THE WRONG TIME?

Roger von Oech, in his useful handbook on creativity, *A Kick in the Seat of the Pants*, describes four roles managers can use to improve their creativity: the "explorer," who finds raw materials for ideas; the "artist," who juxtaposes the raw materials and asks questions to come up with ideas; the "judge," who analyzes and pays attention to gut feelings in order to decide to follow up on the idea; and the "warrior," who fights to implement the idea. There's no doubt we managers are good at playing some, if not all, of these four roles or we wouldn't be where we are. Our trouble comes, von Oech says, when we use the roles at the wrong times.

As experienced managers, we generally know which role we fill most adequately. Therefore it's natural that we move ahead or delay in order to get to or remain in our strongest role. That's not always productive when it comes to generating innovation. If we explore at great length, we may cut short the time for artistic juggling of our ideas. If we juggle for too long, we can't act in a timely fashion. If we judge too quickly, we may cut off innovative ideas. If we take too long to think it over, we may delay decisions unnecessarily. And if we don't think long enough, we act precipitously. As you can see, there are a lot of ifs on the road from "what if" to "what is." Fortunately, a combination of finely practiced intuition and logical analysis can help you know when to delay and when to move on to another role.

PHASE ONE: GET COMFORTABLE WITH YOUR OWN CREATIVITY

Now that you've seen the ways your creativity became blocked in the past, you can move through the CHANGING Process, rediscover your creativity, and put it to work for you. You'll need your intuitive skills to manage the innovative people in your group and help them release their own creativity. I've seen time after time that the best starting point for being a superb manager of innovative top performers is to become more intuitive yourself.

C   CREATE A CONCRETE DESCRIPTION OF THE DESIRED CHANGE.

As precisely as possible, identify the issue that blocks you. If you have picked a fairly general topic such as risk-taking, narrow it down by examining the exact areas in which you are unwilling to take risks. The key here is to be specific.

I had a great deal of trouble getting started on large projects that called for significant creativity. For example, it took me over a year to start working on this book—a year after I first had the concept developed in my mind.

H HONESTLY EXAMINE YOUR MOTIVATION TO CHANGE.

How much do you really want to change? Are you convinced it will benefit you, or is this one of those changes someone else is trying to push off on you? Is it something you think you should do but that you don't really want to do? Be honest and determine how important this change is to you.

I was apt to delay getting started even though I relished the joy of completing a book and sharing my ideas through publication. In my case, it was very important to get past this writer's block because writing is a significant part of my job. Also, of all the tasks I do, writing has the most potential for creativity and I wanted to make it easier and more fun.

A ABANDON THE OLD BEHAVIOR IN YOUR IMAGINATION.

Allow yourself to imagine what your life would be like, if you were more creative. What would you do? How would you behave? Be specific.

I saw myself working at my computer, loving the process of writing, and feeling impressed and pleased with myself for working late and turning out so many good pages of copy.

N NAME THE CHANGE POSITIVELY.

Make the statement as precise and simple as you can, so you can say it to yourself easily and quickly as a reminder of your goal.

For me, the clearest, simplest statement was, "I love to write." Then I elaborated by saying, "I spend over half my free time writing. I feel good when I am writing and I'm proud of what I accomplish."

G   GIVE ATTENTION TO PAYOFFS.

Those payoffs keep your old behaviors in place. By payoff, I mean the benefit that has come your way because of your reluctance to develop your creative skills. Face up to the fact that if some good had not come from resisting the use of creativity, you would have developed it long ago.

Initially, procrastination got me a lot of attention from my dad. If I waited long enough to begin a writing project, he'd lend a hand, and I loved working with him by my side. With his encouragement, I learned to be a perfectionist and got very good grades for our joint efforts. As an adult, still the perfectionist, I delayed starting so that I could excuse any imperfections in my writing by telling myself, "Well, I did the best I could, in the four hours I had."

**I   IMAGINE THE PAST AND
SEE HOW YOU BEHAVED.**

Gather your memories together and imagine that someone treated you the way you wish you had been treated. Feel the pride and sense of ownership you would have had if you had succeeded in being innovative and creative.

My dad was a great resource when it came to homework. Particularly with writing projects, he always used a logical approach and lots of helpful hints and constructive criticism when he helped me. He taught me to be critical and judgmental, not creative.

I can remember back in the sixth grade, my homeroom teacher (whom I adored) asked us to write several poems. I was humiliated, because I couldn't cut loose enough to create any rhymes. In college, I took a creative writing class and again I was convinced that nothing I could do would be good enough.

Now, in my imagination, I'm back in the sixth grade. But this time my teacher is showing us a rhyming dictionary and playing rhyming games with us. Writing poems seems like fun, all of a sudden. Next my dad approves my attempts at creativity in high school and praises a B grade earned completely without his help. Finally, I think of myself in college, tapping away at a computer like the one I have now, able to cut and paste electronically, working away skillfully, easily, and happily.

N   NAIL DOWN THE NEW BEHAVIOR
USING MENTAL REHEARSAL.

How do you plan to react the next time you face a challenge that demands your creativity? Imagine exactly how you'll employ your new behavior.

As I think ahead to a training program I've promised to develop and an article I want to write, I imagine typing my ideas into my computer. I enter them blithely one after the other as they come to mind. I imagine returning to my first draft a few days later, ready to rearrange and consolidate the ideas. By then, my intuition has had a chance to assess the validity of my first thoughts, and I pat myself on the back for moving ahead without delay and for coming up with several ideas worth saving. I look forward to polishing these ideas and adding more in my next writing session.

G   GRADUATE TO THE NEW BEHAVIOR.

Give others a chance to help you and learn from you. Show them that you have overcome a long-term stuck place. Tell stories about it. Share the process so change stops being a major issue and the focus moves to your willingness to drop an old behavior and the support you gave yourself because you deserved it.

I set this change process in action last winter and made a point of telling my staff about the excitement and pleasure I was getting from my new-found ease in writing. When Sarah Evenns, a staff member, told me she'd always wanted to be a trainer but was afraid to stand up in front of a group, I encouraged her to set forth on a similar change process herself. She enrolled in several self-development programs. We exchanged experiences as the weeks went by, encouraging one another, and when a trainer opening occurred, she volunteered for it.

PHASE TWO: MANAGE WITH CREATIVITY

If you're like most managers, your day is fragmented into hundreds of activities that take anywhere from a minute to half an hour each. Of necessity, you must juggle demands on your time to attend meetings, supervise, and check on equipment breakdowns. Maybe, if you're lucky, you're able to set aside 2 to 3 percent of your time for thinking and planning ahead.

It doesn't sound like fertile ground for inventing anything new, but it is. I'll admit that you may not use longer-term creativity very often, because you're not expected to develop new products as technical experts do. Still, as your primary work role continues to surge from managing people toward leading them, you will need the time-saving features and the renewing insights of intuition. In addition, you will want all possible creative contributions from your employees.

STEP ONE: USE INTUITION TO LIGHTEN YOUR MANAGEMENT LOAD WITH MORE INSIGHTFUL DECISIONS.

Intuition, the manager's chief creative talent, is the ability to interpret seemingly isolated bits of information and experiences very quickly to make a practical decision. The complex problems you face as a manager can't always be solved using left brain, analytical, deductive processes. Frequently you haven't the time or available resources to gather all the data required to make careful, well-reasoned decisions. This is when it's smart to trust your instincts. Intuition may be as time saving as switching to a new supplier just before the old one folds or as fortuitous as anticipating the decline in consumer enthusiasm for computer games. It provides you with new ways to see and solve problems and to make and implement decisions.

To develop confidence in your own intuition, make a list of the times it has worked well for you already. The more you see how it has helped in the past, the more it will occur to you to trust it in the future.

Buoyed by your own memories of success, approach your next problem intuitively. Instead of breaking it down into its logical elements, think of the problem as a whole. Program your mind with any available information, then think about the problem divergently by seriously considering any idea that comes to mind rather than discounting or judging it immediately. Apply your imagination and, if appropriate, your five senses as well, to combine and recombine your ideas. With your logic turned off, startling and useful new ideas have a way of popping up unexpectedly. Move isolated bits of data and experience around until, like the pieces of a puzzle, they suddenly resolve into a meaningful pattern.

A technique even beginners find productive is to move on to another task and let your intuition work along on its own. Initially, you may think it's risky to trust your intuition to function independently. That, of course, is just what it's best at doing. While your conscious mind is engaged in the daily demands of your job, your unconscious mind is disengaged to sift and sort, propose, evaluate, and finally suggest solutions to you.

I checked out the effectiveness of my own intuition in an unusual way a few years ago. At Impell, where I often had to shuttle between the second and eighth floors, I made a practice of guessing which of six elevators would appear first. I kept track of the number of times I was right and wrong. With each month my hit rate increased. Within six months, I was 80 percent accurate.

During the semiconductor recession of 1986 and 1987, KLA went through a solid eighteen months of tough times until we finally had a strong quarter of record bookings. Instead of having our standard quarter-end meeting to communicate this financial information to employees, we decided to have a major event. I spoke with Karen James, who plans all our company parties, and asked her if she had any ideas. She said, "Right now I feel rather overwhelmed by the prospect of pulling this together in two weeks, but let me think about it overnight." The next morning she described her unique idea of an "Over the Hump" event, complete with a camel, senior executives in sheik costumes, belly dancers, and the like. The hoopla that resulted was all because Karen let her subconscious work for her overnight.

For most of us, the possibility of handling two things at once is a particularly attractive feature of intuitive thinking. Besides, you needn't use intuition as a substitute for logical analysis. It's not the opposite of rationality, nor is it a random process of guessing. By combining instinct with systematic analysis, quantified data, and thoughtfulness, you'll reach faster and better decisions.

STEP TWO: TURN ON THE CREATIVITY OF ALL YOUR EMPLOYEES.

Frederick Herzberg, originator of the maintenance-motivation theory of management in the 1960s, believed that managers in the ideal work setting would support employees with positive recognition, promotions, and a sense of achievement and personal growth. This is exactly the environment you create as you model the Worth Ethic for your organization, and it will encourage any employee who is already creative.

But what about the majority of employees who feel they are less than creative? You can coax their latent creativity forward in five ways, all of which will increase their self-worth and their self-confidence:

1. Expose them to new ideas. Abandon your old bureaucratic ways and create teams and cross-group task forces instead. Cross-fertilization of ideas and feedback from people with other interests and expertise will spark new insights. Peter Drucker, in *The Practice of Innovation,* says that an imperative of innovation is to encourage employees to look, ask, and listen.

2. Encourage them to speak up. In meetings, use a multiple-option approach to stimulate new ideas. Let people know it's all right to disagree with you. Don't get attached to your own ideas and don't be too quick to choose an approach. Prove you have impeccable motives by never stealing their ideas and never accepting praise that's rightfully due them.

3. Try them out in new roles. The person who can't come up with good ideas in one area may be just great at devising ingenious field tests or marketing approaches. Selling a product idea internally to top management or externally to customers is as important as having the idea in the first place, when your goal is to introduce an innovative product line to the marketplace.

4. Be realistic and vocal about expectations. Admit your own mistakes and tolerate theirs. Encourage them to tell you when a project isn't going anywhere. Explain that if failure is admitted early, it saves funds for the next venture.

5. Give employees as much control as possible over what they do. In a study of 120 R & D scientists from 25 companies, the Center for Creative Leadership reported that 70 percent of the participants cited freedom and control over their work as the most important factors for stimulating creativity.

Essentially, you turn on employees' creativity by investing in them as people, rather than investing in their ideas. In this way you create a climate for innovation. If you are persistent, one of these people may come up with an idea that will support the company for decades to come. At 3M, senior scientists are given time each week to pursue particularly interesting ideas. At IBM the pinnacle of the technical career ladder is the IBM fellow, who has the opportunity to pursue for five years any idea that captures his or her imagination. At the end of that time, the IBM fellow returns to the original work group but retains the prestigious title.

STEP THREE: PROTECTING CREATIVE IDEAS FROM
PREMATURE OUTSIDE INTERFERENCE.

Particularly when you manage a group that's developing a creative product or solution, you take on a responsibility that demands great sensitivity. Kanter outlines three primary tasks for managers of innovative projects: to buffer the team from outside interference, to maintain the group's momentum including redesigning the project, if necessary, to keep it moving, and to insure continuing outside support. You must become what Tom Peters in *Thriving on Chaos* calls an "executive champion—a nurturer, protector, facilitator, and interference runner for as many energetic champions as you can muster."

As a creative manager, you will use your intuition to help head off possible obstacles and interference from outsiders.

You will take the trouble to explain the value of your creative group to people who complain about the chaos they produce. You will harness the chaos so it is as productive as possible. And you'll act as intermediary to get the group whatever resources it needs. Computer time? Travel funds? Laboratory equipment? Whatever they need, you'll get it.

You will also deal with the internal problems that can derail a creative project. You'll hold meetings to keep everyone involved and committed to the team and the project. You'll notice a particularly irksome task and offload it by hiring a willing contractor or getting another group interested in helping out. You'll sense discouragement, perhaps, but revive enthusiasm in some dramatic fashion to remind everyone of the project's importance. Jim Schultz, General Manager of KLA's new product division, meets each morning at 8 A.M. with all managers and once a week with the entire division to share information and encourage results.

These aren't requirements, mind you. They're possible ways you'll spend your time when you use your intuition to enhance your ability to manage. At KLA, we keep our Advanced Technology group in another building, separate from senior management. With this arrangement, we provide a buffer between day-to-day operations and the advanced technology group. Of course this group holds regular review meetings with senior management to ensure that they get input and support, as well as the necessary resources to continue their projects. But these meetings are quite different from uncontrolled interference.

PHASE THREE: SHARE THE BENEFITS OF CREATIVITY THROUGHOUT THE COMPANY

The bigger an organization is, the harder it is to keep creativity alive. In *The Creative Organization*, Karl Albrecht warns, "Growth tends to kill creativity simply because the elephant cannot move as quickly as the rabbit." Still, even an elephant of a company can, in time, be made to turn around. And elephants can run pretty fast when they want to.

STEP ONE: LOBBY FOR SEED MONEY FOR INNOVATIVE PROJECTS.

In budget discussions, urge the company to earmark corporate funds for exploring and exploiting new ideas. Dramatize the need for new product and service lines so that even the most reluctant of your company's bureaucrats admits they have to be developed. To reassure the foot-draggers, encourage the company to set up a monitoring system to cut off unproductive ideas and recommend more funds for productive ones. Then, to reassure engineers that you really want them to use the seed money you've allocated, simplify the monitoring system so that it is free of red tape. An innovative environment flourishes when energy is not spent on paperwork but is invested in creative projects where it belongs.

Sooner or later, foresight pays off. In the 1960s, DuPont recognized the need for new products and started a number of new ventures. Naturally, not every venture succeeded, but by 1982, half of the company's profits came from products started back then, twenty years before.

STEP TWO: REWARD EMPLOYEES' CREATIVE CONTRIBUTIONS.

You get what you recognize and pay for. If you want people to be innovative, reward them for coming up with smarter ways to work. Reward small innovations, not just breakthroughs. Tom Peters points out that innovation "most often comes not from a breakthrough idea but from the accumulation of thousands of tiny enhancements."

One reward that hooks into the Worth Ethic is a dual promotion ladder so that innovators, like managers, can see a long-term career for themselves in the company. Your creative technical experts shouldn't be left out of your company's bonus scheme either, since they contribute to the bottom-line profits of the company just as much as managers do. At IBM, a fellow receives respect and compensation comparable to that of a vice president.

To spotlight employees' innovative product proposals, set up a forum of your most respected people to review them. This will distribute significant glory as well as circumvent the regular, slower chain of command for approval to move ahead. One of the most successful programs to fight absenteeism is that of New York Life Insurance. People who come to work regularly are eligible to win a lottery for $200 to $1,000 bonds. The idea sat neglected for ten years before it was implemented.

Remember to recognize the mavericks in support departments. At KLA, Jack Anderson in Management Information Systems routinely writes complicated human resources software codes over the weekend so that we can use the system again the next Monday. He took over this extra responsibility because he refused to redo the sloppy work done by the previous programming consultant. Instead, he wanted to start over and design more elegant and far faster software programs. To reward him, we gave him several spot bonuses over a year's time, thanked him at the senior staff meetings, made sure his manager and his manager's manager knew about his good work, and recommended him for the next management slot when it opened up in MIS.

STEP THREE: DEVELOP A BROAD PROGRAM TO
HIRE CREATIVE PEOPLE.

Undoubtedly your company works vigorously to hire people with management potential. It can hire people with a creative bent just as systematically. To do so, add creativity requirements to the formal job descriptions for positions that would benefit from this talent. Test for creativity traits during the hiring process. Brandon Lee, a business psychologist specializing in assessments, uses the 16-PF (Personality Factors) test to evaluate potential for practical creativity.

I expect that if you look over the interview feedback sheet that the personnel group provides to hiring managers, you will not find a single request for information on the job candidate's creative talents or inclination toward innovation. Linda Larsen, an employment manager, developed these questions that she finds effective in uncovering the creativity of job applicants: What is the most radical idea you ever had that was implemented? How did you come up with the idea? What did you do to get the idea accepted? How did you develop support? After questions about successful innovation, she reverses direction and asks questions such as: What was the best idea you ever had that you couldn't get implemented? Why wasn't it used? How did you feel about your failed attempts? What would you do differently next time?

STEP FOUR: TRAIN YOUR EMPLOYEES TO USE THEIR CREATIVITY AT WORK.

Creativity courses are effective. They stimulate people's intuition and eventually set them free to do astonishing new things. Tony Merrick, KLA's manufacturing director, attended a course created by Jim Kouzes, then director of executive development at the University of Santa Clara, and Barry Posner, associate professor at Santa Clara. One goal of their "Leadership Challenge" workshop was to enable managers to develop creative and energetic teams by fostering commitment to a noble cause. Back at work, Tony applied the theory in a way that intensified the motivation of his manufacturing team. After he read an article that lauded the new machine his group was building but doubted its completion in time for an upcoming trade show, Tony wrote a letter to the editor stating that KLA would have the machine ready or "die in the attempt." Tony had everyone in his group sign it. He sent it off and then had the finished letter enlarged and posted all over the building. Facing down the analyst's criticism, he created a worthy cause.

Introduce creativity courses to your company and publicize them well, and you will have a subtle but powerful positive effect on your employees' self-perceptions. Tell them that the company expects them to do more than perpetuate what is. Encourage them to make changes and take risks. Managers from Dow Chemical, GM, Hewlett-Packard, and Sears are sent to the Peco River Learning Center, near Santa Fe, New Mexico, where Larry Wilson, director of the center, offers conventional people opportunities for some unconventional experiences, such as crossing the Pecos River on hand-held pulley lines.

Creativity courses also tell employees you want them to develop their intuition. Lynn Chapin and Buzz Noe, founders of Capers of Los Angeles, regularly reenact murder mystery events for corporations in an effort to teach managers to think for themselves. In each "case," the plot is orchestrated to create a multitude of clues and suspects. Then, after the "murder" occurs without warning but with plenty of witnesses, the company managers are let in on the fun and divided into teams to solve the mystery. Courses like these encourage new self-perceptions that are a profound source of human satisfaction for employees who live by the Worth Ethic.

When psychologist Abraham Maslow first talked about self-actualization nearly thirty years ago, only 8 percent of American people hoped to reach this peak. Today nearly 40 percent expect to find self-fulfillment in jobs that make use of their total capabilities and, for many people, that includes their creative potential.

7

THE QUANTUM LEAP
Holding Patterns Have No Destination

*"If you love someone . . . you will always believe in him,
always expect the best of him, and always stand your
ground in defending him."*
—1 CORINTHIANS 13:7

We all get just about what we expect to get out of life.
That's true for companies as well as individuals. A recent study
by Berlew and Hall revealed a 72 percent correlation between
a company's initial expectations and an employee's contributions for the next five years. When a company sets high
expectations and provides multiple opportunities for its
employees, the company and employees alike make technical,
marketing, and production breakthroughs.

The dramatic effect of high expectations was documented
in the Rockaway, New York, district office of the Metropolitan
Life Insurance Company. The manager placed all of his superior salesmen in one unit to give them an environment that
would stimulate performance. Then he challenged them to
achieve two-thirds of the total volume of premium sales made
by the entire agency the year before. Predictably, the performance of the superior salesmen increased dramatically and
sales by the group of weaker salesmen declined. More sur-

prisingly, the average group increased its sales significantly. The assistant manager in charge of the average group refused to accept the district manager's assessment of his management capability or his agents' sales abilities. He challenged his staff to outperform the "super" staff, saying they lacked nothing but years of experience. The group lived up to his expectations. Although they didn't reach the dollar volume of the more experienced group, the average salesmen increased their productivity by a higher percentage than the superior salesmen.

Studies show that the chance to grow, learn, and improve skills are among the top five reasons employees give for accepting a new position. Bob Lo Presto, senior partner of Korn/Ferry International, the world's largest executive search firm, says, "High potential employees are more willing than ever before to change companies in order to be part of something important. They want to believe they are making worthy contributions to the group. They want to fulfill their own expectations for growth."

BROAD BENEFITS DELIVERED

Companies that expect employees to take on new challenges and develop new skills in steep growth spurts do so because they hope to improve employee satisfaction and corporate productivity. The National Alliance of Business warns that " . . . an undereducated work force is an unmotivated and unproductive one."

To increase employee satisfaction, companies provide on-the-job coaching and training programs. Such programs improve skills that lead to promotions and pay increases. The Rand Research Report of 1986 found that formal training boosts an employee's earnings for over thirteen years. Managerial, professional, and technical training increases employee earnings by 14 to 16 percent. These tangible rewards also create intangible benefits as they create an atmosphere in which employees are excited about future opportunities.

Joani Selement, a freelance writer working on a research project with me, asked top executives from twenty-five successful high-growth Silicon Valley companies to account for the most abrupt leaps they made in their careers. One-third said moves to challenging new jobs supercharged their careers; one-third cited formal training programs that improved their leadership behavior; and one-third described the importance of a mentor or coach who gave them regular feedback and took an active role in their development.

Both group and one-on-one programs can motivate employees and expose them to new ways of working. But neither option works until managers first change and grow themselves, to show they believe others can do the same. That belief, clearly communicated, is what prompts employees to believe that they, too, can change.

Joanne Marlow, head of her own $2 million fashion design company in Evanston, Illinois, coached her assistant to become a showroom salesperson. Marlow is a powerful role model because of her long experience and personal success. At twelve, she earned $300 a month selling patterns by mail. She is now twenty-one. Today her assistant-turned-salesperson dreams of opening a clothing distribution company with her boss's help, and Marlow lets her work part-time while she gets the company going. If you, as a manager, have developed your abilities over the years, you no doubt find it entirely reasonable to expect your employees to learn new information and gain new skills.

I know I do. As a first-year graduate student studying psychology, I saw the movie *My Fair Lady*. Professor Higgins became my role model in the sense that he showed me how someone who invests a little time in people who are motivated can help them make leaps in their work and personal lives. Although I detested his cool aloofness toward Eliza Doolittle, I was awed by his ability to help shape a highly motivated person. I remember watching the movie with gooseflesh prickling my arms and thinking that I wanted to have this sort of impact on people, too.

To improve productivity, the Tennant Company, maker of industrial floor-maintenance equipment and finishers, invests $50,000 a year on thirty-five classes for 1,800 workers, including many "soft" offerings like "Managing Personal Growth," "Listening," and "Positive Feedback." As a result, its manufacturing rework time has plunged from 44,000 hours a year in 1979 to 5,000 hours a year in 1988. During the same period, products damaged in shipment have been reduced by 87 percent, while problems during equipment installation have been reduced from 24 percent to 7 percent.

I believe that the biggest productivity gains come simply because self-confident employees are not afraid to speak up and seek help when a problem develops. People who stay focused on solving problems rather than hiding errors, placing blame, or hogging glory, are far more likely to produce startling and innovative insights and quality products.

OBSTACLES TO QUANTUM JUMPS

If you're not sure people can develop and use new skills in a short period of intensive learning, that negative expectation, too, will spill over and influence your employees to devalue their growth opportunities. To achieve the advantages of your employees' potential, you must surmount the obstacles created by your own attitudes and your experiences in the past.

Do you expect your company to offer you a significantly different and challenging job in the near future? Do you have plans to develop new skills and talents? Do you enjoy growing, changing, and learning new things? If you answered no to any of these questions, you've begun to identify potential obstacles standing between you and your ability to transform your employees into more satisfied and productive workers. Remember that no one changes until you change first. Let's look at the possible obstacles to making your own vertical leaps and subsequently supporting your employees' efforts.

YOU FEEL POWERLESS TO CREATE BREAKTHROUGH
OPPORTUNITIES FOR YOURSELF.

You believe that top management has you pigeonholed. At one time a KLA executive had me pigeonholed just because I was in human resources. He thought all human resources people were far too willing to spend the company's profits. I needed to turn his opinion around so he would free up resources when I needed them. To do so, first I gave him an opportunity to explain his perspective, and I really listened. Then I told him that I intended to prove his pigeonholing was incorrect. Every time I saved the company money, negotiated a good contract, or had some other positive bottom-line impact, I sent him a note about it. About four months later he stopped me in the hall and pleaded, only half jokingly, "Stop the notes!"

Time and again, you and your employees have come back from training programs pumped up with new ideas only to find the organization or your boss resisting your proposal—even when the company sent you to the course. New ideas meet resistance because putting them in action so often means changing job content, power structures, and ways of doing things.

In the first place, change is generally painful. So, since you and your employees aren't necessarily encouraged to change, you feel you're just as happy staying the way you are and where you are. In your mind, you have yourself pigeonholed in your present job and see no way to move out. You hear a lot about correcting problems but very little about optimizing strengths. You aren't encouraged to take your strengths and combine them to propel yourself forward.

Yes, you can get out of a pigeonhole if you want to. But some people don't want to. I once interviewed a candidate for a general manager position who said, without a blink, "I think most of us stay pretty much the same throughout our adult lives." He told me he had consultants working with him in his last job, where the compar.y thought he was technically brilliant but too autocratic in his management style. He said he felt he was still very much the same and, in fact, didn't see the need to change. He hoped that KLA would be able to accept him the way he was. Moreover, he felt that once a company labeled a person, it didn't change its mind and that, in the end, the person came to believe the label was a correct assessment.

That candidate for general manager, like a lot of others who believe in pigeonholes, was speaking mostly of himself. If you feel you are pigeonholed in your present position, consider the possibility that you are unmotivated rather than unable to change. Let's be honest. If you're typical, you probably resent the idea that you have room for improvement at this stage of your career. You may feel very excited about the idea of growing and changing, but when real situations occur in which you could lead in a new way, you're probably inclined to back away from the change. The old ways work well enough, you think to yourself, ignoring the clear link that exists between your willingness to grow and your employees' willingness to grow. Your lack of interest becomes theirs as well. Once you acknowledge the power of your expectations on your employees, you'll recognize your immediate need to gain new information, new skills, new insights. If you don't create breakthrough opportunities for yourself, neither will they.

YOU BELIEVE THAT PERSONAL CHANGE AND GROWTH
ARE HARD WORK, HIGH RISK, AND NO FUN AT ALL.

You know that breaking an ingrained habit or learning to react in a new way isn't easy. In fact, you may never have experienced change as an exhilarating experience. Many of us are unwilling to make the struggle required to try new, unproven ways of operating. Possibly we fear failure. Often we don't see the necessity for taking the risk of change. However unpalatable the payoffs of our present mode are, we at least know what to expect and we have experience dealing with them.

As a manager, you can help your employees feel that risking a sudden change is worth the effort. Whether people sit in a college classroom or a corporate training program, they learn only what they think they need to know. If you let them know exactly what you expect from them, however, tell them how they fit into your plans for the organization, and give them on-the-job coaching, they will realize for themselves what they need to learn. When nuclear engineer Sarah Clemons found herself after twenty years in a dying industry, she became a stockbroker. She received a great deal of specialized training before she took up this new profession. But the breakthrough came long before the training sessions began, Clemons says. Her chance was activated by a boost in self-worth that came with an opportunity to manage the family funds—actively and productively. From this experience, she knew what she needed to learn from the stockbroker training program.

Incidentally, a leap is sometimes not an external change in career path or capabilities. A breakthrough can be a dramatic change in perspective. In eighth grade my daughter, Catherine, had to face up to some important choices and the life-style options that would naturally come from those choices. Up to that time, in the small school she attended, her grades had always been average. But no one had to know that. Moving to a much larger school, Catherine found herself excluded from the honors classes her friends were in. After the first quarter's grades came out, she said, "You know, I think I want to be on the honor roll." I asked her what she would have to do to get there and she said, "First of all, I need to decide that I can do it, and I think I can, and then I must make it a priority." Sure enough, the last two quarters of school, she was on the honor roll.

Growth can be invigorating. I once needed to build a team out of a group of eight confrontive and often combative men, each of whom headed up a different department. Getting them together was difficult, and getting them to agree on anything was impossible. I tried one-on-one discussions to persuade them to behave and concentrate on the team objectives in the general meetings. Yet the meetings still deteriorated into table pounding or everyone talking at once. One month I decided that if they could do it, I could do it, too. Never mind that I had always been taught I shouldn't behave that way.

At home, I practiced banging on the table and talking very loudly. In the next meeting, I put those techniques into practice to get their attention. The men were so surprised by my new aggressive methods, they recognized how irritating their own abrasiveness was. As a result, they settled down to work as a team. My confidence surged, my self-worth soared—and so did my leadership capabilities.

Looking back, I recognize a recurring pattern of self-growth. First I take a new job that brings with it all sorts of changes and external pressures: long, intense hours of learning new responsibilities; new schools and friends for my daughter, considerable travel to get hands-on exposure at outlying offices; and the risk involved in establishing my credibility in a new office, a new company, even a whole new field. Out of those pressures I form opportunities to learn. I am exhilarated by my new competencies. Next, I settle into my job, refine my ideas, and install them in the organization. The writing phase is last, when I attempt to share my ideas and implementation methods with other people. What is your growth pattern? How do you break free of a stuck position and make a genuine change? How do you inspire your own fervor and change with a consistency that amazes the people around you?

PHASE ONE: ACTIVATE THE *CHANGING* PROCESS

Naturally, this business of increasing employees' willingness and expectation to change must begin with you first. Right now, I'd like you to review your last nine months to a year, and look for times you deliberately said no to a challenge. How about that computerized message system you meant to get trained on? Or that extension course you promised yourself last summer? Have you attended a company-wide program that sparked a new idea, yet delayed experimenting with it? Whether you've refused to try on a single new idea or an entire management trend, you're inhibiting your ability to lead others out of their pigeonholes.

C CREATE A CONCRETE DESCRIPTION OF THE DESIRED CHANGE.

Do you need to change your basic attitude toward the possibility of growth and change? Or is it your budget or your training targets that need changing? Whatever area you need to work on, describe it in detail.

I was once an eager, excited management trainer, which is how I got my start in human resources. But today I often feel discouraged. It seems that people don't honestly change that much. Increasingly I notice this of myself, too. Yes, I've made incremental changes over the past three years. Still, I don't notice any particularly monumental ones. And I'm ready for one.

H HONESTLY EXAMINE YOUR MOTIVATION TO CHANGE.

Your head may say growth is important, but what does your heart say? Get in touch with your honest feelings.

I'm highly motivated to change this discouraged part of myself. I'm willing, even when I consider the risk and upheaval it will bring to my life. I know it will not only allow me to grow more rapidly myself, but that it will also allow me to once again facilitate major shifts in other people.

A ABANDON THE OLD BEHAVIOR IN YOUR IMAGINATION.

Think of your personal and organizational goals, then imagine how easily you'd reach them in the absence of your present behavior or attitude toward developing potential.

———————

I used to put myself into a new job or totally new field with great regularity. But I've become increasingly more inclined to devise reasons to turn down jobs rather than consider moving from KLA. Now where do I find excitement in my job? What do I do to propel myself into action now that I am working in an excellent company?

In my imagination, I see myself as I used to be, early in my career—turned on by the possibility of growth, both mine and that of the managers with whom I work. I hear the excitement and enthusiasm in my voice. I feel my aliveness, as I mentally and emotionally tackle new concepts and lead others into explorations of themselves and their full possibilities. What fun it would be to change jobs and recapture those thrills. But no, I am at the pinnacle of my career. I can go to a larger company as the top human resources executive or I can go to a huge company as a second-level human resources manager. But neither move would be much of a stretch. I already have competency in all the technical areas and I've worked with a senior management group. What used to propel me forward was a sense of stepping up the career ladder. I have to look beyond the old motivations that propelled me to action.

———————

N NAME THE CHANGE POSITIVELY.

Brevity's the ticket here. Keep your statement crisp and to the point so you can emblazon it in your consciousness. This is a statement of who you are becoming.

For me, this means, "I am now creating new break-through opportunities in all parts of my life."

G   GIVE ATTENTION TO PAYOFFS.

What's kept this behavior in place? How did holding down employee development or holding back on your own growth help you? Surely you got some reward for your old way of thinking or doing.

Letting go of my high motivation to grow and to help others grow gave me the opportunity to add a number of new skills to my professional repertoire. For example, I wouldn't have had the time and energy to dig so completely into com-pensation systems and devise programs that reinforced team efforts if I had remained locked into my former identity as a trainer and a coach. I also would not have put aside the time to write this book if I had been focused on my short-term growth. My time would have been spent in other ways. With less upheaval and less risk in my life, I had the chance to develop more balance. I was rewarded by a fair amount of peace, daily routine, and financial predictability. I was also less exhausted. Those aren't bad rewards, for a while.

I   IMAGINE THE PAST AND SEE HOW YOU BEHAVED.

Suppose you'd had more positive learning and growth experiences yourself or that you'd been more successful at helping employees remove their rough edges or adopt new skills. Imagine how you would be today and how you'd feel about developing potential.

In my twenties I was very interested in health, and I leaped through an entire growth cycle within an eight-year period. It began when I avoided surgery by taking vitamins and eating carefully, and culminated with a book and guest moderator spots on a daily TV program. I moved quickly from proving to myself that good health was essential, to promoting healthful life-styles to my social work clients, to advising the general public on health regimens and exposing health frauds.

Now, at 41, I am completing another phase as a human resources professional. In a decade I've broadened my job from management training in the classroom, to directing human resources projects, to developing and implementing my own programs, to sharing my ideas about how to manage the new work force. I still feel very invested in this field because in it I have found my life mission. I want to help transform organizations so that the quality of life for millions of corporate employees is improved every day. Looking at my past, I believe I made useful though sometimes traumatic moves.

Somehow I need to get back on a steep learning curve where my growth is once again coming in big bursts rather than small new skill increments. I see that is as much a state of mind as something that needs to change in the outside world.

I imagine myself in the past again, still taking some risks but with more forethought and better planning. At Impell, I had four positions in three years and at one point I filled two positions simultaneously. What if I hadn't wanted to get ahead quite so much? If I'd made fewer changes and taken longer in each position, could I have arrived at the present without stress and chaos?

I imagine living without calamity. I think that if I'd been cautious I wouldn't have grown very much. For me, the risk of the unknown and the terror of unpredictable crises accelerate learning. Apparently my present reluctance to risk the financial and emotional security of my present job are holding me back. I realize that I'll stagnate if I can't tear myself loose from the false security of stock options and an executive's paycheck.

N   NAIL DOWN THE NEW BEHAVIOR USING MENTAL REHEARSAL.

Move ahead, in your imagination, to the challenges you'll face tomorrow, next month, and next year. Imagine yourself making leaps with your new attitudes and behaviors. Think through the decisions you'll be facing so you're ready when the time comes.

Looking to the years ahead, I see scores of new ways to transmit what I've learned and to increase my own learning. I see myself setting new long-range career goals, finding the courage to risk and be stretched, and expanding the arena I'm playing in.

I see myself taking a leadership role with human resource people from other companies and sharing my ideas as a consultant in executive development. I see myself spending time with human resource managers from companies in other parts of the world. I recognize that my own creative spark needs feeding, so I see myself signing up for workshops where I'll come in contact with world leaders in my field.

G   GRADUATE TO THE NEW BEHAVIOR.

Model a new behavior and you'll help others acquire it, too. Let your employees see you developing your own potential and enthusiastically supporting employee development in your group. Show them you want to help them be their very best.

At KLA, I developed the Individual Leadership Program. Within my own department, I coached Jean Farr toward her career goal of heading up a human resources function of her own. I helped to broaden her competency by giving her new responsibilities in her first year at KLA. I took a chance on her ability to learn a lot in a hurry, and I let her know why I'm willing to take these risks with her. She responded by putting her heart and soul as well as her mind into her job.

Outside KLA, I created an independent consultancy to help others achieve a Worth Ethic. Within the scope of my expertise, I'm closing in on my goal of improving the quality of life for significant numbers of people. We've all taken this motto to heart: Grow as if your career and your company depend on it, because they do.

PHASE TWO: CREATE BREAKTHROUGH OPPORTUNITIES

Your employees look to you as both a resource and a role model on how to succeed within your organization. Put that admiration to work for you. Become sincerely and personally involved through one-on-one coaching and your employees will begin to make all sorts of internal, technological, and career breakthroughs. Very quickly, you'll find you are helping yourself while you are helping them.

STEP ONE: SHARE TEACHING EXAMPLES FROM YOUR OWN EXPERIENCE ON A REGULAR BASIS.

Coaching is a potentially powerful tool for facing up to bothersome problems and passing on information, skills, and values from manager to employee. The people who work with you want to know how you got where you are and how they can get there, too. When you sit down with them, one-on-one, you give employees the chance to tell you what they are doing and what problems they are facing. You, on the other hand, have an opening to share your experiences and to take notice of their performance, too.

Most managers delight in helping another human grow because, in the process, they help and sustain the work group. But you may resist taking on this role because you know it's going to take time and skill. You may not be certain about your return on your investment. The fact is, however, that you've no choice in the matter. You fill the role deliberately or by default. Once you forfeit your chance to help employees make breakthroughs, you doom your group to stagnation or the constant churning of employees in and out of your organization.

KLA's top management read about Intel's one-on-one meetings and liked the idea enough to implement them in our company. It was easy. Executives started having one-on-ones with those who reported directly to them. Within six to twelve months, even those managers who'd never before met individually with their employees were holding regular meetings. With no pressure, just the power of these positive examples, our employees began to get better direction and have more contact with their managers.

One word of caution: A one-on-one session is not a lecture forum. It's an opportunity for both of you to ask questions and share concerns. Rather than appear as a critic or teacher, establish the fact that you and the employee are on the same team and can leap ahead as a team. If you still haven't learned to listen, now is the time to learn. You'll want to provide constructive feedback that will help your employee succeed with you and for you.

STEP TWO: REACH A MUTUAL UNDERSTANDING
ON THE DEVELOPMENTAL AREAS
THAT NEED ATTENTION.

In general, use a coaching program to improve employee performance, prepare employees to assume greater self-direction and broader responsibilities, or ready them for promotion. Specifically, you and your employee must agree on what the employee will be working on, how you'll rate the employee's improvement, and what opportunities may result. Don't rush this process; it's fundamental to motivating the leap you want to see your employee take. Set the goals, then work out an action plan together.

Take particular care that you focus on genuine developmental goals. This is not the place to take a critical approach toward performance problems. Good performers, in particular, will be demotivated by a session that focuses on improving weaknesses. If you haven't added to your own pack of management skills recently, I urge you to pay special attention to the enthusiasm good performers bring to a developmental program that focuses on building strengths. Your success at getting employees to leap ahead personally and professionally clearly depends on your persistence in improving your own skills as a manager, regardless of how good (or bad) you think you are.

STEP THREE: SCHEDULE REGULAR ONE-ON-ONE
SESSIONS TO MONITOR PROGRESS.

How do you ensure that your employees will progress toward their developmental goals? To begin with, your support is of benefit all by itself. Even top performers need assistance as they reach their upper limits so that they won't backslide. Research by management consultant Harry Levinson, previously a business professor at Harvard University, shows successful CEOs can accurately assess their effectiveness as leaders, but many managers who fail to make it to the CEO level lack this ability. Still, they're afraid to ask for advice. They fear that a confidant will interpret their request for help as an admission that they can't fill the job, or, worse yet, will pass their concerns on to top management.

In one-on-one meetings, you become the trusted confidant who will give employees the feedback they need in order to grow. Develop their trust by talking about what they're doing right. Suppose your employee runs an idea past you, or asks for your assessment of a plan. If you pick at the flaws, you alienate that person. Instead, work together to refine the idea or plan. This is not a mere semantics issue, but a fundamental difference in approach. A critic is an enemy to be defeated. A coach is a master of the trade who is willing to pass on what he or she has learned to a willing apprentice.

PHASE THREE: INTRODUCE A COMPANY-WIDE PROGRAM TO PROMOTE BREAKTHROUGH GROWTH

Max DePree says the lasting reward of being a leader is "having the opportunity to make a meaningful difference in the lives of those who permit leaders to lead." DePree is chairman of Herman Miller, the Zeeland, Michigan, furniture maker that is one of *Fortune* magazine's 10 "most admired" companies in America.

Once you share your success in one-on-one coaching, the idea will catch on. Then the coaching process itself can serve as a role model for developing formal programs to promote breakthroughs in employee skills, insights, and career paths.

STEP ONE: EXPAND THE COACHING PROCESS INTO A MENTORING PROGRAM.

Mentoring is the ideal way to introduce the wisdom and experience of senior people to younger high-potential employees. Jerry Wilbur, vice president of the Service Master Company in Downers Grove, Illinois, says, "Mentoring is to the organization what the sequoia is to the forest." His analogy is particularly apt because the sequoia gives back 80 percent more than it takes from its forest environment. While senior employees certainly help along the careers of more junior employees, they also receive benefits of their own. The junior employee becomes a handy resource, a natural ally, and part of an informal information network.

Traditionally, mentors have been high achievers with a

strong urge to help others move ahead. Their rewards were, for the most part, psychological. Mentoring was not part of their formal job. Increasingly, formal mentoring programs are being structured by companies such as Johnson & Johnson, Bell Laboratories, and Merrill Lynch. These companies recognize that savvy executives can help managers grow and that this is a particularly effective way of developing high potential managers. Many high-growth Silicon Valley companies have also learned that mentoring is a good way to indoctrinate new employees into the company's work culture and values.

Here are a few suggestions for moving ahead: Begin simply. Assign all new employees to a buddy a level or two above, to help them get acclimated to the company ground rules, expectations, and values. Once that's underway, develop courses on how to mentor. Such training will help people to become more effective leaders whether or not they choose to be mentors. The training should include advice on how to encourage and praise employees, how to promote other people's strengths within the company, how to provide career counseling, and how to build high trust and a sense of shared common interests. One of the things that makes a mentor relationship work well is the chemistry that results when people share common interests and common values. Consequently, the training should also address ways to locate potential mentors and build rapport with them. Employees, including first-level and middle managers, almost always need to learn how to attract and work with mentors.

STEP TWO: CREATE A HOTHOUSE CLIMATE
FOR CAREER DEVELOPMENT.

Careers, like orchids, thrive in an intense atmosphere of constant attention. A career is not the same as a job. By the time we are managers, we know that. But for many employees the first step in growth is simply to get some sense of what they really want to do.

A career development training program is useful, particularly for hourly employees and people who are just out of college. Typically this sort of get-in-touch-with-your-own-career-aspiration kind of workshop can be done in one day. Then, several weeks later, everyone meets again for perhaps a half-day session to learn about the kinds of jobs available throughout the company, and the education and experience required to get into those positions. At that time, participants are provided with a resource list of people who are willing to be interviewed about their actual job content. The process of creating and distributing the list builds awareness that the company expects all employees to help one another with career development.

To keep their careers blooming, employees need to know the different skills and personal qualities necessary in their current job and other jobs of interest in their organization. A good program for providing this information is a checklist of skills and qualities. Managers can use this to prioritize the required skills, evaluate employees' competence, and determine the developmental needs of people who want to get ahead. Employees who want to work for other departments can use the same checklist to get meaningful information from managers there.

Naturally, managers need a training program on how to do priority and skill evaluations, so that they present the information in an upbeat, positive fashion. As in coaching, the positive approach that focuses on strengths is most effective. Areas of weakness should not be attacked and criticized. Rather, they should be addressed as areas that employees need to develop over the next year or two in preparation for making a leap forward. Employees who show a lack of interest or an inability to work effectively in one group may do well in another. But managers can't facilitate those positive changes if they don't know how to identify open positions and whom to contact in other groups.

Employees, also, need training on self-evaluation of their skills and their leadership qualities. They should be able to compare their self-evaluations with the manager's evaluation, to get some feel for their "black holes," those development areas they had not previously seen. Sometimes they will disagree with their manager's evaluation. In that case, they need to know enough about themselves to decide who is right. Finally, they must be taught how to change the image they project, if they truly believe the manager's assessment is wrong. Without a realistic sense of what they do well, how they appear to others, and what opportunities they can aspire to, employees' careers will wilt.

The programs I've outlined will undoubtedly generate excitement and a variety of resources to keep careers blooming. But on-the-job training is also necessary. Frederick Herzberg, professor of psychology at Case Western Reserve University, was to my knowledge the first person who wrote about job enrichment and encouraged managers to build it into their organizations. In an interview study Joan Selement and I conducted of managers who made career leaps, one-third reported that their significant growth spurt came on the job. These managers found themselves in a hothouse and they met the challenge because their managers believed in them and trained them, then and there. Essentially, that's what on-the-job training does in every instance. It provides concrete proof that the manager expects the employee to grow and change.

STEP THREE: DEVELOP AN INDIVIDUAL LEADERSHIP
PROGRAM FOR MANAGERS.

For any company, the ability to develop and maintain management talent is not just desirable, it's critical. Losing trained managers and failing to bring new leaders speedily up to par means the company can't stay ahead of its competition. Moreover, if managers feel plateaued and leave in search of job satisfaction or more glorious titles, the company suffers from the cost of replacement. The Individual Development Program I designed identifies the strengths, shortcomings, and interests of managers. It formalizes the coaching and CHANGING Processes. Because the program benefits high-potential managers, plateaued managers, and managers with new areas of responsibility, it signifies neither elitism nor stigma. Regardless of their situations, managers come out of the Individual Development Program with a realistic idea of what their capabilities are and how their talents fit within the company. In ten half-day sessions spread over a six-month period, the manager gets an assessment of his or her leadership and management skills, an identification of areas where growth is needed, and coaching and counseling through the change process.

The assessment phase begins with an empathetic discussion of the manager's present job demands, responsibilities, rewards, and difficulties. This is followed by a survey of ten co-workers and in-depth interviews with the person's manager and one or two other significant people in his or her work group. Naturally, the managers both dread and look forward to the assessment results. This first uncomfortable step is the real hook into the program. The surveys and the subsequent interviews are specific, personal, and direct. From this data, we are able to identify areas where change is needed. Managers I have worked with are sometimes greatly surprised to learn what co-workers see as weaknesses. They may have not seen those drawbacks at all. Possibly they've even perceived them as strengths. Although at first they frequently respond defensively to this information, it helps them uncover the life patterns that created impediments to their growth. Once managers know what pieces of their background influenced the particular behaviors, the process of change becomes easier.

Coaching and counseling through the change process most often focuses on strengthening the manager's interactive leadership skills. We try to identify a long-term project that the manager can use to try out his or her leadership. Then we set interim goals and review progress over the course of the program. Basically, we follow the CHANGING Process. Meanwhile, we keep the manager's manager constantly aware of changes that take place and his or her role in reinforcing those changes. As the one makes a commitment to change, the other must make a commitment to recognize and reward change.

By the end of the program, managers have learned which parts of their management style work for them, they've rehearsed new skills and ways of behaving, and ideally they've leaped ahead—all without moving to a new company!

What is needed, before and beyond training, mentoring, and coaching, is a clear expectation of where the person is heading. As my high school geometry teacher said when he taught me to draw a straight line on the blackboard, "Put the chalk here at point A, but always keep your eye on point B."

8

THE OWNERSHIP INCENTIVE
An Open Hand Signals Friendship

*"A system of values is the content
for the workings of any economy."*
—Marilyn Ferguson, *The Aquarian Conspiracy*

Who arrives early and stays late? Who rejoices when the company turns a profit and sticks it out when times are bad? Who invests heart, mind, and money in the future of the company? You guessed it. Anyone that committed is bound to be an owner. Ownership is the key to the Worth Ethic. So companies is search of employees who act like owners are rewarding them like owners. They're paying for performance and sharing the profits.

The New Age accent on personal responsibility must be connected to financial payoffs. Psychological rewards are fine, but material rewards are the universal measuring stick people use to tell how well they are performing. At a time of first-, second-, third-, and fourth-level managers and cramped managerial cubicles, people can't always brag about their titles or office space. But they can always point with pride to the profits they generate and enjoy. Pay as substitute for meaningful work raises little more than a whiff of interest in today's worker. But pay as recognition and reward for work well done can tighten the resolve of workers to continue to work well and hard.

Ownership builds corporate strength. Publicly held companies that are at least 10 percent employee owned outperform competitors by 62 to 75 percent. Firms where employees own a major portion of the company generate new jobs four times as fast as other companies. Firms owned outright by employees are 150 percent as profitable and have twice the growth rate of other companies.

Ownership doesn't have to be a legality to be a psychological reality, either. In the wallowing steel industry, for example, two companies that treat workers like owners stand out as consistently profitable and productive. Worthington Industries has never laid off a permanent employee in its thirty years of making steel, and its absentee rate is 20 percent below the industry average. At Worthington, profit-sharing adds, on average, 40 percent to employee paychecks. At Nucor Steel Corporation, in Charlotte, North Carolina, where weekly gain-sharing bonuses often exceed 100 percent of base pay, employees produce 980 tons of steel per employee, over two and a half times the industry average. These companies show that the lack of employee commitment to productivity, not the high rate of union wages, caused America's overall steel industry to flounder.

At Lincoln Electric of Euclid, Ohio, where the performance bonus system is based on a complex formula that pays for piecework production, quality products, excellent merit reviews, and company profits, productivity exceeds the industry average by 250 percent.

At Visible Changes, Inc., a Houston-based chain of sixteen hair salons, sales exceeded $1.5 million in 1986, with revenue from retail products four times the industry average. Employee turnover was one-third the industry average. One reason for the low turnover at Visible Changes is that its hairdressers typically earn compensation almost three times the industry average. Another reason is that everyone gets 15 percent of their pay in profit sharing.

Members of the new work force expect to work in genuine partnership with the company, so they fit right into these kinds of companies. But 75 percent of all employees see no direct link between their work and their pay. Some partnership. A majority, 68 percent of employees, believe their productivity would go up if pay were tied to performance. Edward E. Lawler, research professor of management and organization at the University of Southern California, reports productivity increases of between 15 and 35 percent when incentive pay systems are installed. Yet ordinary compensation and benefits programs simply reimburse employees for their time worked.

THE FAILURE TO CONNECT PAY TO PRODUCTIVITY

From kindergarten through college, American youngsters work for rewards. They earn grades in school, medals in scouting, and paychecks at McDonald's. By the time they enter the full-time work force, their positive reaction to the "dangling carrot" is almost instinctive. At Proctor and Gamble, a profit-distribution plan has distributed profits to workers in direct proportion to labor costs since 1887. Yet companies fail to make a clear connection between productivity and pay in their compensation plans more often than not. A Conference Board study of 491 companies revealed a mere 11 percent had profit-sharing plans, only 8 percent had all-employee bonuses, a minuscule 3 percent had group productivity incentives, and fewer than one percent had group cost-control incentives.

A survey of 359 major U.S. companies by Towers, Perrin, Forster & Crosby (TPF&C), widely respected compensation consultants, disclosed that 84 percent of the respondents use merit, not productivity, as a standard for determining pay increases. TPF&C found 41 percent of the companies do not believe their employees see a link between pay and performance and 44 percent do not believe their employees know how their pay is set. They confirmed findings of a 1983 Public

Agenda survey that 77 percent of employees see no direct link between their work and their pay.

Finally, the Opinion Research Corporation of Princeton, New Jersey, surveying over 108,000 employees between the years 1980 to 1986, found an astonishing 43 percent of employees didn't believe good performance would lead to a pay increase. They're probably right. Eight people who saved their parent company $100 million in taxes, back in 1981, would certainly agree. They got bonuses of only $3,000 each—for generating more than $10 million in tax savings apiece.

In my own experience, I found the level of effort required to perform well went largely unrewarded. In my first four corporate positions, I was asked to set up entirely new functions, gain credibility, and show immediate results. Yet when salary increases, bonuses, and stock options were awarded, I got about the same as a person at my level who had had the same job for three years. Yes, the people with three years of experience in the same position worked hard and were good at their jobs, but they had to exert nowhere near the level of effort required to start up new functions. I got excellent work experience, but I remember realizing that if my performance had been average instead of outstanding, the actual difference in my salary would have been only $1,000 less a year, or about $50 a month after taxes. The difference in performance required that I put in ten extra hours of work nearly every week.

Managers I meet at conferences and workshops across the country complain to me about the poor performance of their employees. When I ask them what rewards would follow exceptional performance if they got it, they have no ready answer. Their employees believe, of course, that nothing would happen if they worked harder, or faster, or smarter except that their managers' lives might be somewhat easier. Why should they be concerned with performance standards when mediocre performance is rewarded and high performance is ignored? Why work hard if you don't get paid for it?

Pay for performance makes sense. It works. Among U.S.

employees, 68 percent believe their productivity would go up if pay were tied to performance, according to a Louis Harris survey made in 1983. Another survey, this one by the Public Agenda Foundation, reports that 73 percent of workers believe they work less hard because they do not get incentive pay. But few companies act on that knowledge. Instead they pay people small merit increases each year. There's little difference among paychecks received by the most outstanding performers and the average people.

ROADBLOCKS TO CHANGE

Why aren't managers more generous, when generosity produces such a good return on investment? What obstacles stand in your way as you try to build a model compensation system that rewards and reinforces strong performance by your employees? What are the blocks to generosity? They're four in number, and they all come from the same mountain range of personal insecurities: We believe money's too scarce to be shared. We view compensation as an expense not a profit generator. We're afraid to tell people what they're really worth or pay them what they really deserve. We fear the loss of our own authority and prestige.

MONEY IS SCARCE.

Why don't we stimulate productivity by paying for it, clearly and tangibly? Frankly, we don't because most of us are a bit stingy and insecure. We believe we will never have as much money as we want or need. Usually we picked up these attitudes in childhood by listening to our parents argue about money or yearn for things that they couldn't afford, and we got the idea that almost no one except the very rich ever have as much money as they need.

As long as we treat money as a scarce resource, we find it hard to be genuinely generous. We may want to be generous.

Our friends and associates may believe that our heart is in the right place, but in reality we're a bit mistrustful. It's hard to be generous with something that, deep inside, we honestly believe is quite hard to come by.

Our belief in scarcity, particularly of money, is pervasive and one of the most destructive beliefs operating in most companies. It's destructive because we fail to motivate optimum productivity when we don't pay for performance. It's destructive because we find it difficult to truly share the wealth with the very people who make the company's financial success possible. Moreover, if we're blocked by this fear, we're probably not too comfortable sharing financial information with employees. We don't want to open the books, justify expenditures, and explain why some people are more valuable (that is, paid more) than others. Still, that's what employees need to know. With sufficient financial information, people become committed to adding to their paychecks through bonuses, profit-sharing, and other compensation programs that link their performance to the company's performance and tie both to their pay.

COMPENSATION IS AN EXPENSE, NOT A PROFIT GENERATOR.

Sometimes we managers get myopic, keeping our eye on the company's earnings per share. We begin to look at incentive programs as an expense, not a means of increasing profits. Take the management at Continental Airlines for example. Continental turned its financial picture from red to black between 1983 and 1986 by getting employees to identify with the company's fortunes. In 1985 alone, pilots saved about $5 million in fuel costs by flying at slower, more fuel-efficient speeds. Management gratefully split the savings with them, fifty-fifty. Then management lost sight of the fact that profit-sharing programs generate more profits. It stopped believing that increased pay would motivate sufficient performance improvements to offset the increased costs. Rather than distribute profits visibly to employees, it began to use profits to fund growth and earnings. By the first half of 1987, experienced mechanics and pilots had departed. By June 1988, in spite of mounting costs from mergers the airline was again providing its pilots and first- and second-level officers incentive bonuses in the form of gainsharing.

THE NEWS MAY BE BAD.

None of us likes to be the bearer of bad news. Still, if we're going to operate from the Worth Ethic viewpoint, we need to be sufficiently honest to provide poor performers with the kind of feedback that will motivate them to improve or find a more compatible position.

I see managers give reasonable increases to people who are performing below the level of reasonable expectations, ensuring the status quo by communicating to them that mediocre performance is okay. In the process, they handicap their ability to recognize strong performers. If we gave no increases to poor performers and significant increases to our best performers, we would actually come closer to paying for performance. Instead, we protect ourselves from change and upset, and protect our employees from the financial consequences of their behavior.

Why do we pay our worst people more and our best people less than they deserve? What makes us afraid to tell people what they're really worth? The Public Agenda Foundation tells us that 73 percent of U.S. workers don't work as hard as they used to. I think we've brainwashed ourselves into thinking we can't light a fire under that 73 percent who have dwindling productivity or exclusively hire that highly productive top 27 percent. I think most managers believe their employees can't do much better than they're doing, or that they themselves can't find better people to replace their poor to average performers.

Several years ago, I had a manager recommend a pro forma 5 percent increase for an employee whose productivity had declined badly over the previous six months. His performance didn't warrant termination, but I objected to a raise. We talked about what a raise would say to the employee at that time, and he revised the raise to a minimal 3 percent. This got the employee's attention. The next year his performance turned around, and he earned an outstanding performance rating, a 12 percent salary increase, and a $4,000 bonus.

Why, indeed, should we assume that poor performers will leave the company if not given a sizable yearly salary increase? And why assume we should tolerate them if they don't improve? Poor performers put more work on good performers, reduce the overall productivity of the group, and demolish morale. The Public Agenda Foundation reports that over half of all employees believe that their companies "carry" poor performers.

At Lincoln Electric in Ohio, new employees struggle so hard to meet peer standards that, according to compensation expert Theodore Cohn, they call the first two years there "purgatory." To be a permanent worker (and eligible for a bonus) new employees must be voted in by their fellow workers. The co-workers are tough to please because the bonuses they get depend on high productivity from the entire team. Still, the newcomer's learning effort pays off in the end. Both pay and productivity at Lincoln Electric are twice the average.

At KLA, top performers get rewards and poor performers get the message. The bottom 15 percent of employees receive no salary increases or stock options. Because these policies are not kept secret, KLA employees know what the company thinks of their performance by looking at their pay stubs. Incidentally, this is an unexpected benefit of an open compensation plan—as employees become discontented with how the company perceives them, they move on. The overall quality of our work force improves without any additional or unusual effort.

WE COULD LOSE OUR PLACE IN LINE.

In the future, compensation will come to depend on genuine recognition of each person's contribution to the total organization rather than a superimposed hierarchy. But this will take some getting used to. From the time we first entered the work force, it was simply understood that managers make more money than the people who work under them. Rosabeth Moss Kanter, a Harvard Business School professor, observes that pay has traditionally been an indicator of a job's rank within the corporate hierarchy rather than an indicator of the actual value of the contributions a person makes while filling that job. If, suddenly, our top performers earn more than we do, we fear we'll lose our authority over them. No wonder we're reluctant to reward and reinforce strong performance by compensating employees in relation to their contribution to the company. That might mean paying for a person's value regardless of age, or years of experience, or even if it meant the employee would be paid more than we are.

Once we acknowledge that performance-related pay helps rather than hinders our managerial goals, we no longer need to fear we'll lose our own place in line by increasing an employee's pay. Pay becomes a significant motivator and reward for behavior without detracting from our prerogatives. Performance doesn't have to be measured on an "I win-you lose" basis.

Throughout this book we've looked at various ways to think about and act toward employees, ways to make people productive at work by inviting their whole selves to work— minds, muscles, and hearts—by meeting their need for connectedness, for belonging to a family of sorts. Compensation is just one more way to recognize a person's worth to the company and in the process boost the organization's competitiveness in the marketplace. It's quite possible to mesh our reward system with a Worth Ethic management style. We can pay for teamwork, innovation, quality improvement, or any other behavior we want to motivate.

If you're in a position to change or influence the external compensation policy of your company, and if you select intelligently from the vast range of available rewards, you can use compensation to reinforce the Worth Ethic philosophy and culture.

PHASE ONE: CHANGE FROM WITHIN

First you need to adopt a more generous personal attitude toward money. If you change your internal attitude you'll be able to change your external behavior. You need to let go of any dissatisfaction you personally have about money and any beliefs you hold about the scarcity of money. In the process, you'll learn how to compensate justly your employees' contributions to the company.

C   CREATE A CONCRETE DESCRIPTION
OF THE DESIRED CHANGE.

Perhaps you are too tight with your budget when it comes to distributing it to others in salary increases and bonuses. Maybe you're unwilling to care enough to take the heat that would come from refusing to pay for poor performance. Specifically, describe the change in attitude you'd like to make.

———————

A few years ago, I worked with Glenda Middleton, the president and founder of a computer housing manufacturing company. Glenda brought me in as a consultant to help her on her leadership skills, in particular to improve her ability to build employee loyalty to her company. The company was then about eight years old and had grown quickly from a start-up to a middle-sized company. In the early years turnover had been nominal, but now turnover was increasing at all levels. Naturally, this troubled Glenda.

In just a few hours together we uncovered some leadership issues that Glenda could work on. But one of the problems underlying the company's turnover was that the compensation system was not competitive. Glenda had profited greatly from being tight with money, both personally and in building the company. Yet she could now see that some of her decisions about money were shortsighted. Turnover is itself very expensive. Recruitment costs often total $5,000 to $10,000, plus the cost of relocation when that is necessary. In addition, the cost of lost productivity can be as much as half the person's annual salary during the changeover. "Obviously, I need a more realistic way to see money," Glenda agreed.

H HONESTLY EXAMINE YOUR MOTIVATION TO CHANGE.

Are you convinced that generosity with company profits can, in fact, stimulate the productivity of employees and result in further profits? Does generosity appeal to you?

Glenda was determined not to become so generous that she made poor financial decisions. She had some serious reservations about changing her attitude toward money. "I don't want to give away the store, Kate," she complained. Still, Glenda was eager to find a more balanced perspective—and cut down on turnover.

A ABANDON THE OLD BEHAVIOR IN YOUR IMAGINATION.

Allow yourself to imagine what life would be like if you weren't dragging your insecurities about money around with you.

This was fun for Glenda. She played with the idea of being generous with money, handing out a bigger allowance to her teenager, and going on a clothes spending spree for herself.

In the business area, Glenda had more trouble imagining any new generosity. From the beginning, her compensation manager had advocated salary increases, equity adjustments, and higher merit increase guidelines; she'd resisted his urgings for the past four years.

I suggested she try a worst-case scenario—to imagine what she would feel like if she ended up in bankruptcy. Glenda imagined that her two adult children plotted to take control of the company once they realized how much the company was worth. She imagined they would suck her dry or tuck her in a convalescent home. I asked Glenda to play out these soap opera situations one at a time and see how they could be avoided. When she started to laugh at these worst-case fears, we talked about the choices her children had already made in their lives, and the fact that they were maturing into reliable adults. She got increasingly comfortable with their competence in handling money, so I turned her attention to the present: What was likely to happen if she loosened her hold on expenditures at the plant?

Glenda imagined that two of her most productive managers had asked for hefty raises. She imagined that she had met with her compensation manager and human resources director and together they had devised an employee ownership program. She imagined that right from the beginning she had concurred with her board of directors when they encouraged her to instigate profit sharing. As she thought how each of these changes might have motivated employees to work a little harder and with more dedication, Glenda began to see that she might have built a different type of company. With high dedication and low turnover, the company she was creating in her imagination could have the same profitability even though its expenses were higher. Once she admitted this possibility, she was ready to move ahead to the next step.

N   NAME THE CHANGE POSITIVELY.

Condense your intended change into a statement that you can post in a convenient place as a reminder of your new goal. Make it positive and succinct.

Glenda said to herself, "I happily increase employee compensation packages to improve productivity. I have a more balanced view of money."

G   GIVE ATTENTION TO PAYOFFS.

The positive reinforcements from a certain behavior aren't always apparent at first. Give yourself a few moments to see what benefits came to you as a result of your present attitude toward money. For example, does being tight with money help you keep your organization significantly below budget? Or do you perhaps use the possibility of promotion and the salary increase it brings to justify your long work hours to your family?

For Glenda there were definite payoffs for being tight with money. Her frugality allowed her to go straight to college out of high school and let her live in a dorm, away from home, which was something she really wanted to do. Once she graduated with an MBA in business, she won a spot on an internship program with a major corporation, and she received well-earned kudos there for her ability to handle a budget. She owned a late model car and had the down payment for a town house by the time she married. In other words, she enjoyed material payoffs and a sense of pride in all areas of her life because of her frugal attitude toward money. Until now.

I   IMAGINE THE PAST AND SEE HOW YOU BEHAVED.

Examine the beliefs that were operating in the past and how they affected your behavior. Then consider how you would have acted differently, without your present attitude about money.

———————

Glenda never felt she'd had enough money. Because she grew up poor, she dreamed of college and saved for it the way some teenagers dream and save for the senior prom. Only her dream didn't take up three or four months of her senior year. She saved two-thirds of whatever she made, from seventh grade on, and the remainder went for essentials only. The success of her early struggles to save money gave Glenda a lot of satisfaction. "But I get pretty grim about spending money for anything that's not absolutely necessary," she confided.

I encouraged her to imagine she had grown up with a huge allowance and parents who insisted on paying her way through school. She cooperated with enthusiasm, building a fantasy world for herself as a youngster, growing up with all the money she wanted and knowing she could always get more. She said she experienced a quickness to act, once the money constraints were removed from her thinking. As she imagined being an ordinary person, not spending frivolously but just spending most of what she had, knowing there would always be adequate money and good jobs in her future, she felt her anxiety drop. She wondered aloud, "Do you suppose all this worry about money isn't so smart after all?"

Turning her attention to her management intern experiences, she recalled a project in a customer service department in which the women who answered the phones were significantly underpaid. At the time the unfairness of their compensation had troubled Glenda. But she also knew the budget constraints of the customer service department. Now, in her imagination, she recommended huge salary increases for these women to provide them with salaries that were competitive and equitable. She saw their productivity increase because their efforts were being recognized and rewarded at last. Glenda allowed herself to think that the sales manager dropped by to see what was different and to tell her that customers were telling their sales people about the huge improvement in services in the past two months. With my prompting, Glenda allowed herself to imagine she received a $500 bonus for improving the productivity in that department.

As a young manager, before she started her company, Glenda squeezed real value out of every expenditure she approved. "I'm a budget monster at home, too," she admitted. She imagined allocating money for a year-end party at work and long-needed new furniture for her living room. She imagined the lift she would get from these expenditures. Everyone, herself included, might feel less driven and more productive.

N NAIL DOWN THE NEW BEHAVIOR USING MENTAL REHEARSAL.

Look to the future, anticipate problems you'll face that will challenge your new perspective, and imagine using your new attitudes about money skillfully and successfully.

One problem Glenda recognized immediately was that she'd built a company in which many people besides herself were tight with money. She'd been a strong role model in this respect, so penny-pinching was definitely part of the company culture. Glenda rehearsed the meeting she would have with her board of directors, going public with her new attitude toward money, and heard herself telling them frankly that she now agreed with their earlier stand. The company needed profit sharing.

Next Glenda imagined that she held a series of meetings to explain to managers the need for greater generosity. She'd hired the managers, in part, because they were a tightfisted lot. Some of them would be reluctant to make the change. So she imagined how she would assemble the facts to show generosity can pay off in greater commitment, lower turnover, and higher productivity.

At my insistence, Glenda also turned her attention to her personal finances. She thought about how she squirreled money into savings accounts rather than investing any of her hard-earned money on riskier ventures. She imagined "taking a flyer" on occasion or (and this was difficult for her) withdrawing several thousand dollars to take a real vacation. In the end, she reminded herself that money wasn't "finite." She could always earn more.

G GRADUATE TO THE NEW BEHAVIOR.

Put the new you to work. Begin to act on your new generosity and set an example for your managers and employees.

Glenda looked at the compensation program in place at her company and saw three changes she wanted to make. As an immediate change, she broadened her managers' role in giving out spot bonuses. This was the one part of the compensation program she still liked. However, under the current setup she had to approve every spot bonus over $25. Managers had to justify the award in writing, wait for approval, and expect to defend their nomination in a brisk debate with Glenda almost every time. In other words, she'd made the program nearly unworkable. She wrote a memo saying every year 2 percent of the payroll would be distributed in spot bonuses given to employees at the time of an outstanding achievement. This would give managers a way of recognizing and reinforcing superb performance when it occurred. This revised program was her first step in drawing a direct relationship between what people made and what they achieved for the company.

Since Glenda now saw that profit sharing made a lot of

sense, her second action was to begin the process for installing it. She also set up a task force to come up with ideas for an incentive bonus system for which every employee would be eligible.

Her third action was to schedule monthly meetings with her managers and semiannual meetings with her employees to talk about the shift in the company's culture and the compensation programs that would emerge. She let everyone know they could expect to see the new changes begin with the next fiscal year, just four months away.

Phase One is now complete—you're learning to be more generous with yourself. It's time to move to Phase Two and practice being generous with others.

PHASE TWO: MANAGE WITH GENEROSITY

You know that people who are treated like owners feel like owners and work like owners. And you know that by rewarding caring behavior, you put Worth Ethic ways of operating in vogue long enough to see results. Here are two steps you can take to model generosity in your compensation practices.

STEP ONE: GENEROUSLY REWARD YOUR EMPLOYEES BASED ON THE RESULTS THEY ACHIEVE.

Just as responsible friends or parents withhold their approval for destructive or wayward behavior, so you, in adopting the Worth Ethic, need to give an honest compensation message to someone who delivers poor performance. If you don't do that, you're being uncaring and self-defeating as well. Only by withholding salary increases from poor performers will you have funds available to reward great performers generously.

At KLA, we grant merit raises from 0 to 15 percent rather

than the customary 3 to 8 percent. Then, to clearly connect effort and reward, we set aside a pool of 1.5 percent of our payroll to use in awarding spot bonuses to employees who achieve extraordinary results.

Once you have the money, be generous to good performers in as many ways as possible. Install cross-functional bonus systems to reward collaborative efforts—Tom Peters recommends that we use our bonus money to reward people in other departments who work with us to get things done.

STEP TWO: PLACE FAIR MARKET VALUE
ON YOUR EMPLOYEES' SKILLS.

Pay for knowledge is the most satisfactory kind of performance incentive available to you, according to a survey of 1,598 firms by the American Productivity Center (APC) and the American Compensation Association (ACA). Among those companies who pay for knowledge, 89 percent are happy with the system.

Employees who have cross-trained on different machinery can assume someone else's job in an emergency. They can mean the difference between hiring too many people in slack times and getting behind in busy times. Therefore, cross-trained employees are highly valuable to your organization. Employees who have taken on two or three additional responsibilities since they were hired, or who have significantly improved their skills through training and experience, have also escalated their value in the job market.

Yet we rarely offer cross-trained employees an unsolicited raise. If they go out and find another job, we may match the offer. But we lose their skills and experience in any case— workers rarely return to the fold once they've begun to search for a new job. Why don't we manage with an open hand and let employees' salaries keep pace with their fair market value?

We think we're getting a bargain, until we're left with unfilled positions. We think we're getting a bargain, bringing in a new hire whose limitations we don't know yet. Our employees shouldn't have to change jobs to get a well-deserved raise. The best bargains of all are employees who qualify themselves for raises, get them, and then are remotivated to further add to their value to the company.

PHASE THREE: DESIGN A COMPANY-WIDE DUAL-COMPENSATION SYSTEM

A company's compensation program, like its promotion policy, is a powerful motivator, since it rewards certain behaviors and types of performance, and continues to reward them week after week.

The ideal pay plan for a Worth Ethic company is a dual system. Employees receive their base pay plus funds from multiple incentive plans that reflect their performance achievements. You need to select program elements that will draw a direct connection between high performance, ownership behavior, and the objectives of your organization.

STEP ONE: VOLUNTEER TO WORK WITH YOUR COMPANY'S HUMAN RESOURCES MANAGER TO INSTALL AN INCENTIVE PROGRAM.

Compensation programs that pay for hours spent at work have lost their effectiveness, now that the work ethic is outmoded. The human resources specialists in your company undoubtedly know that. But they also know that because compensation is a sacred part of most companies, that change will take time. They expect progress to be slow. You may be surprised to discover they are waiting for a line manager like yourself to walk in, ready to lend support and willing to get involved in their dreams of creating more flexible compensation programs.

To the extent that a company compensates people for behaviors that show they care about the organization—its products and services—the company is paying for what it needs. Companies that pay for performance share profits based on individual contribution. There's a fine flip side to flexible compensation plans, too. Companies that offer pay incentives and bonuses based on a combination of individual and corporate performance can offer lower base pay. In this way companies that distribute flexible dollars when times are good also enjoy a lighter cost of labor burden when times are tough. Employees share in the misfortunes as well as the fortunes of the competitive marketplace.

STEP TWO: REVIEW APPROPRIATE INCENTIVE PROGRAMS.

Incentive plans can reward quality improvement, productivity, profits, better service, or any other results of employees' efforts. Let's examine the options available to you. The 1,598 firms surveyed by ACP and ACA reported that companies used nine different kinds of incentives: Pay for knowledge; earned time off; gain sharing; small group incentives; profit sharing; individual incentives; salaries; lump-sum bonuses; and recognition. Three-quarters of the companies surveyed used at least one of these systems, and at least two-thirds of the companies who used these programs were happy with them. Recognition programs such as "Employee of the Month" awards, even when accompanied by small bonuses, seemed to do the least to motivate good performance. In general, incentive programs work best when they are used strategically to accomplish very specific goals and are rewarded for team efforts on the basis of a well-publicized bonus formula.

Short-term incentives: These programs target a goal you want to reach quickly. U.S. businesses spent more than $10 billion on vacations, banquets, trips, and other profit-sharing prizes in 1985, up 50 percent from 1980. Use one of these incentives when you know exactly what you want to have happen, how much you can afford to spend, and how you will handle success when it comes. At Mita Copystar of Hasbrouck Heights, New Jersey, a travel incentive campaign promoted sales over the short term and product loyalty over the long term. A 15 to 20 percent increase in business more than offset the $1 million cost of the program.

Incentives can be very low cost and short range. Some companies take a cue from the Japanese and include daily motivational tactics as well as incentive and bonus programs to keep employees involved at work. In St. Louis, Missouri, workers at a hardware company became eligible for a drawing, one prize per twenty-five workers, if they made it to work on time every day for a month. With a perfect record for six months they were eligible to draw for a television set. Absenteeism and tardiness dropped dramatically.

Spot bonuses: To clearly connect effort and reward, you can set aside a pool of dollars to use in awarding spot bonuses to employees who achieve extraordinary results. Spot bonuses sometimes take the form of a check, sometimes a trip, a dinner for two, or a unique gift. At KLA we set aside 1.5 percent of our payroll for this purpose, and that means nearly half a million dollars for performance awards for our 1,000 employees each year.

Piecework bonuses: If you are targeting increased productivity as opposed to net profits, you need to improve the volume and quality of every employee's work. Consequently, you need to include everyone in your program. This can be done by paying for piecework on a manufacturing line, but it's inappropriate in most Worth Ethic environments because of the cut-throat competition it creates. Pay for piecework promotes an "I win-you lose" attitude. It sacrifices team spirit and cooperation, unless it is combined with team incentives and stock options that focus on group as well as individual performance.

Product royalty bonuses: You can keep your engineering people tightly focused on profits by offering them product royalty bonuses. At 3M, compensation at senior levels has been linked to the percentage of sales that come from new products introduced in the previous couple of years. At Memphis Software Company, programmers receive bonuses based on the sales of the programs they develop. The more popular their programs are, the higher their bonuses. Such plans motivate employees to keep development costs low and to design products that really meet customers' needs.

Pay-for-knowledge or multiskill-based pay: This system pays for the number of jobs an employee is capable of performing. As the employee's skill base goes up, so does his or her pay. Especially where employees work as part of a team, the pay-for-knowledge or multiskill-based pay system helps productivity, improves quality, and decreases job turnover by increasing employees' job flexibility. Typically, at the entry level, pay increases are made as employees acquire the skills required by the team. Once every team skill is learned, employees are paid at the higher "team rate" and are eligible to learn skills needed on other teams. Employees are paid at the highest level, the "plant rate," when they can perform every job in the facility.

Worth Ethic companies like pay-for-knowledge and multiskill-based pay plans because they reinforce the belief that employees are their most important resource. People with a variety of skills are more valuable to the company, have more job security, greater job satisfaction, and therefore greater feelings of self-worth. At Wal-Mart, each department is managed as a separate business, with each employee responsible for ordering, merchandise display, and customer service. This nurturing environment pays off in loyalty and low turnover: about 40 percent of the company's managers started out as hourly trainees.

Gain-sharing: This plan pays a monthly bonus for the gains achieved over the previous month. Where individual contributions are hard to assess and employee cooperation is desired—which is most places—try using a gain-sharing plan. Manufacturing plants within GE, TRW, and Motorola find the plan encourages workers to work as teams to cut labor and material costs and to share their ideas for improving how work is done.

Profit-sharing: At KLA, where the effect of individual performance on total company profits is fairly easy to see, we use profit-sharing plans and like them. However, the larger a company is the less these plans actually motivate daily behavior. Since they focus attention on longer term performance by the company, and since employees don't get a very large proportion of the total distribution, their function is mostly to make a symbolic statement that the company shares some portion of its profits with employees.

Still, the symbolic function is significant. In a survey of *Industry Week* readers, 96.3 percent said they are in favor of profit-sharing plans, 84.5 percent said they believe these plans improve employee performance, and 86.3 percent said they believe the plans improve employee motivation. In addition, profit-sharing plans alleviate employee concern that their efforts are simply earning profits for shareholders.

Management by Objectives (MBO) bonuses: Companies that motivate their managers' performance by setting annual objectives reward them with bonuses in proportion to the extent they've met those objectives. MBO bonus programs for managers provide a way to reward top performers with significantly higher pay than poor performers. In some companies MBO bonuses constitute as much as 50 percent of the manager's total annual pay package.

Deferred stock bonuses: One method used by 15 percent of very large companies (those with more than $500 million in sales) is to reward deferred stock bonuses that vest over a number of years, provided long-term goals are met. At Shannon & Luchs, a Washington, D.C., real estate brokerage company, division heads earn 10 to 25 percent of the net profits for their division. Because these division managers hold the reins that control profits in the company, sales and profits are high.

Stock option and stock ownership plans: At present, over 10 million U.S. employees own some portion of their company's stock. Such plans deliver measurable feelings of ownership to employees and measurable advantages to companies. For example, Denver Yellow Cab drivers bought their company out in 1979, and by 1984 they had repaid their bank loan and turnover had dropped from 200 percent to 20 percent. In 1957, Lowe's Companies, a home improvement chain, had 700 employees and just a few stores. Now it has 260 stores and 7,000 employees who own 30 percent of the voting shares of the company. In general, public corporations that are at least 10 percent employee-owned outperform other companies by 62 to 75 percent.

STEP THREE: GET APPROVAL TO SET UP A PILOT PROGRAM.

Your compensation package is the glue that holds caring ways of working and operating in place long enough for them to show results and get integrated into the company. The pilot effort will crystallize your ideas and, if well done, prove your case.

First, plan your objectives. Do you want to motivate greater effort or stimulate risk-taking? Obviously, different objectives demand different approaches.

Basically, you have a choice of individual and group incentives. Individual incentives are appropriate when personal effort alone will achieve results or when each member of a team effort can operate independently. Because the results are not dependent on others' contributions, a team of salespeople will respond enthusiastically to awards based on sales figures, just as long as they have a reasonable chance of reaching their targets. On the other hand, individual incentives frustrate employees whose achievements depend on true teamwork. Because the progress of a development team depends on the contributions of every person on the team, members will work more productively for a group bonus that everyone shares.

You'll need to choose specific short- and long-range goals. If you want employees to use participative management styles that result in quality products and services, then reward those people who use teamwork and collaborative skills successfully. Monthly and quarterly prizes can decrease absenteeism and tardiness in manufacturing workers. Individual and team bonuses, sales commissions, pay for piecework, and travel awards will boost individual effort and, appropriately devised, encourage team efforts as well. Profit sharing can boost employee morale when the company's doing well and when it's not doing well cut labor costs while saving jobs. Determine whether managers or workers control those results so you reward the right people.

Second, establish the eligibility and performance criteria for the plan. People need to know whether or not they're included and what's expected of them. Consistency in design is the most important element here. You'll want to reward the behaviors you need at a level sufficiently high to make a difference.

Third, set up the funding formula. People need to know the percentage of their total compensation at risk under the plan. Decide when the rewards will be delivered—that is, annually, quarterly, or deferred—and who will administer the plan.

Over time you can vary the mix of your total compensation program to reflect changes in short-term goals, employees' responses, and general market conditions. Whenever you introduce a new reward, be sure to define the precise criteria for winning it, keeping guidelines clear and simple, and then publicize the criteria.

KLA's compensation program is flexible in approach as well as in the percentages we award to individual contributors. All employees receive profit sharing, which ranges from 1 to 10 percent, with an average of 5 percent. Spot bonuses account for as much as 10 percent of an outstanding employee's compensation. MBO bonus plans for managers and executives range from 10 to 50 percent, depending on level. Stock options, after a five-year vesting period, account for 25 to 150 percent of base salary, again depending on the employee's level as well as his or her performance.

At KLA we are always open to innovative compensation ideas. For example, we designed a mileage/milestone program to motivate and reward the entire KLA 2020 product development team of thirty-five engineers if they produced the KLA 2020 system on schedule. It gave motivated workers a way to prod the small minority of unmotivated workers to stay after hours, come in on weekends, and work through lunchtime and dinnertime so they'd all win the team award. At the same time, we gave stock options to everyone on the team, with the level of award directly proportionate to their contributions. As a result, KLA finished the 2020 on schedule and the team bypassed the usual downturn in morale (and resulting turnover) that comes with completion of a major project. They celebrated the project's completion for a week in Hawaii with their spouses or friends, all on KLA.

As a manager, do you give lip service to the idea that people are important to your organization? Or do you believe that employees are, indeed, your most important asset? If so, reward them generously. You will discover, to your infinite good fortune, that they will live up to your belief in them. Two-way generosity is the natural product of the Worth Ethic.

9

THE MIND-BODY CONNECTION
Balanced Work Styles Create Peak Performance

*"Overeating, overworking, every imprudence
is a draft on life which health cashes in
and charges at a thousand percent interest."*
—F. G. WELCH

People need to deal with their worries, fears, and stress, otherwise they become worn out and unproductive. That's the conclusion of a study of 2,000 managers over a five-year period, conducted by Fernando Bartolome and Paul A. Lee Evans and reported in *Harvard Business Review.* "What happens out of the office affects employees' performance," says Carlene Ellis, vice president of administration at Intel Corporation in Santa Clara, California. With little family support available, the new work force requires a whole network of fringe benefits—wellness programs and support services—to keep them on the ball and on the job.

Health of mind and body are critical to sustain peak performance in any endeavor. Top athletes train their bodies to deliver all-out effort and train their minds to visualize a perfect performance. They recognize the influence of the mind on the body and the necessity of a strong body to produce what the mind can conceive.

Raoul Montgomery offers a Transcendental Meditation (TM) program to employees in his Detroit Chemical manufacturing company. He credits TM with some hefty changes in his company, including fewer employee grievances, easier contract settlement with the Teamsters Union, a 73 percent decrease in hourly workers' sick leave, as well as a 120 percent increase in sales and a 520 percent increase in profits. To support the Worth Ethic, we, too, must recognize the mind-body connection.

THE HEALTH-WEALTH CONNECTION

Direct health care costs devour 39 percent of net earnings at the average *Fortune* 1000 company, according to *The Wellness Report*, and those costs are still rising. Stress-related illnesses cost businesses at least $33 billion a year, and stress claims account for 11 percent of all workers compensation disease claims. Drug abusers cost business about $30 billion a year in lost productivity. In addition, industry spends $700 million a year for recruitment costs to replace unhealthy workers, and $87 billion in health insurance premiums for employees, retirees, and dependents.

Indirectly, out-of-balance life-styles create further waste for the corporation. Stressed-out people find their creativity and decision-making capabilities blocked. Stress-related compensation claims total approximately $150 billion a year. Imagine the missed opportunities and delays that result because nearly 500 million people annually do not make it to work. Fifty percent of hospital patients over the age of forty-five land there because of their unhealthy life-styles and 80 percent of contemporary deaths are caused by six life-style factors (smoking, high cholesterol, high blood pressure, obesity, alcoholism, and lack of exercise). Faced with statistics like these, visionary managers establish reliable wellness networks to promote the mind-body connection.

WELLNESS AS A CORPORATE PRIORITY

Companies make employee health a priority through the use of various wellness programs which are "proactive," that is, preventive rather than remedial. Some programs are as simple as providing free blood pressure tests or barrels of apples for mid-morning snacks. Some are as elaborate as the company fitness center at Rolm Corporation, in Santa Clara, California, which has lap and exercise pools, a parcourse for runners, tennis and racquetball courts, weight rooms, a gym for basketball, volleyball, and badminton, and an indoor Jacuzzi, steam room, and dry sauna.

At Stevens Real Estate in Lawrence, Kansas, employees are encouraged to work out on trampolines while they listen to sales training tapes. Employees at Central States Health and Life Company of Omaha are paid up to $150 a year to attend aerobics, nutrition, and stop-smoking classes. At Safeway Bakery division in Oregon, employees participate in aerobics and a laugh clinic aimed at teaching them to be more playful. They also enjoy a color TV in the non-smokers' section of the company lunchroom, paid for by the cigarette machine in the smokers' section. Many companies let employees tag an extra 15 minutes to their lunch hour if they spend it at a company exercise class.

Almost all U.S. companies with more than 800 employees contribute to company bridge tournaments, baseball teams, bands, parties, and picnics. In Santa Clara county, the heart of Silicon Valley, almost 10,000 people play on company baseball teams each spring. At Steelcase, the world's largest manufacturer of office furniture, employees have a 1,100-acre recreation center, a health program that includes stop-smoking clinics and stress-reduction seminars, a child-care referral service, and free counseling by staff psychologists and social workers. Mazda Corporation in Flat Rock, Michigan, has a $1 million fitness center with weight machines, exercise bikes, a simulated cross-country ski unit, and facilities for golf, base-ball, volleyball, running, martial arts, and aerobics. Plus a twenty-team basketball league.

These wellness programs show that companies are increasingly interested in their employees' health and happiness. Are they producing the hoped for results? Yes—people are healthier when their companies show an interest in their welfare. The Canada Life Insurance Company, with 1,400 employees, saved $300,000 a year by reducing absenteeism after they set up an employee recreation program. Another research study compared absences of employees who took part in fitness programs with those who did not. In one program, the fitness group was absent 3.5 days compared with 8.6. In another program, the difference was 4.8 to 6.2 days. Canada Life also attributed a 13.5 percent decrease in turnover to the recreation program. Control Data Corporation, in Minneapolis, found employees who exercise have 30 percent fewer hospital days than those who don't and nonsmokers have 18 percent lower medical claim costs.

It's logical that health monitoring programs decrease illness, absenteeism, and turnover. But it's curious, isn't it, how taking part in such simple activities as a lunchtime brown bag program, a hand of bridge, or a game of volleyball actually translate into wellness?

Recreation programs work because they help to control stress. Craig Finney, associate professor of recreation and leisure studies at California State University, conducted research that showed performance drops when people are understressed (that is, when their skills are underused and they are bored) as well as when they are overstressed (that is, when they work under a high workload and become frustrated). This finding was confirmed by a University of Michigan study of employees in twenty-three occupations. Finney's research showed people become stressed and their performance decreases when they lose autonomy. He theorized that simple recreation activities would help them regain control of their lives for a time and consequently have a positive influence on their productivity. His theory proved correct: A group spending just 10 minutes playing games after a stressful task outperformed by 300 percent a group that did not play games.

The positive influence of this modicum of control is remarkable and reproducible. Once employees perceive they can take control of even a small part of their lives, they are able to adopt a different perspective on problems. Rather than endure and internalize their aggravations, and make themselves sick in the process, they begin to express and release their feelings.

Neglecting the physical well-being of employees is like neglecting to check the weather before you go to the beach. You can't sunbathe in the fog. And you can't expect employees to maintain enthusiasm for work when they lack the mental and physical energy to work. Naturally, praise, recognition, making a difference, and all other aspects of the Worth Ethic contribute to people's positive outlook. But first you must empower people to deal with their problems. That means you must make the mind-body connection a personal and then a corporate priority.

BLOCKS TO WELLNESS

Unfortunately, too many of us wait for a heart attack or other physical crisis to focus our attention on what we're doing to our bodies. Up until that time, we're inclined to take our health for granted. As a result, we usually take our employees' health for granted, too. Our attention is more commonly focused on bringing in a project on time, keeping abreast of changes in our profession, or simply keeping our jobs. Let's examine in closer detail those obstacles that keep us from taking better care of our bodies.

GOOD HEALTH ISN'T ON OUR PRIORITY LIST.

I was struck by Denis Waitley's self-description in *The Double Win*, because it's so close to how I see other managers viewing good health habits: "I used to look at my body much as someone views his second car—an older clinker that was good for transportation." Waitley's was a 1933 model, with a half-inflated spare tire and a carburetor running with a little too much cholesterol in the fuel lines. He figured this "1933 Waitley" would get him from birth to death, with maybe an occasional tune-up and, if things got really bad, a valve job. For fuel, he used bean burritos, french fries, banana Moon Pie, Twinkies, Milk Duds, and strawberry shakes. He never thought about trying unleaded or premium stuff. After all, it was only something to run on and the environment was so polluted anyway. Is Waitley's old attitude similar to your own? Are you intent on driving your "clinker" until it falls apart on you and forces you to make health a priority in your life? Most of us neglect preventive health measures out of a sense that they're not really necessary, until it's too late for preventing.

WE HABITUALLY RUN ON FAKE ENERGY.

How many times have you vowed to quit smoking, eat and drink less, or get more exercise? Those activities would increase our actual energy levels, yet we continue to rely on coffee, cigarettes, and candy to give us a false energy boost instead.

The problem with false energy is that it comes with built-in negatives. There's caffeine in coffee, nicotine in cigarettes, and sugar in candy, all of which set our wheels spinning in neutral instead of in drive. Psychologist Robert E. Thayer, a professor at California State University, Long Beach, compared the energy, tension, and fatigue levels generated in college students when they took a walk or ate a candy bar and found that a ten-minute walk delivered longer and better results than the candy bar. The walks decreased tension and increased energy; eating the candy bar delivered a short-lived energy boost but increased tension at the same time. Unfortunately, caffeine, nicotine, and sugar are addictive, so it's hard to give them up, hard to set a good example, and hard to get other people to give them up, too.

WE ACCEPT OUR OUT-OF-BALANCE LIFE-STYLE AS NORMAL.

We think it's necessary to work long hours in order to get ahead. In *Workaholics,* Marilyn Machlowitz accuses employers of saying they want employees to have outside interests and pretending they don't want workaholics, when in reality they continue to encourage workaholic tendencies. A Korn/Ferry International study, reported in *Fortune* in April 1987, found that a senior-level executive at a *Fortune* 1000 company works an average of fifty-six hours a week (up from fifty-three in 1986). With that kind of example to follow, we're convinced that we have to work long hours to get promoted. Even if we have nothing critical to finish, we come early, stay late, and return on weekends to put in "face time." One ambitious manager I know went so far as to buy a second car to park in his slot on weekends to impress anyone who drove by.

Seduced into believing that long hours and hard work will bring us success, we've steeled ourselves to forego the pleasure of contact and intimacy with our families. We've opted, instead, for the promise of fulfillment later on. We've deluded ourselves by thinking, "Later on, there will be time for fun and games with the family. Later on, we'll travel and strengthen our family bonds." Unfortunately it gets easier and easier to thrust off the demands of our hearts and put off our families until "later on" becomes "too late."

There's another, more honest way to achieve a balance between work and play than to think we can work forty years, then play twenty years, and be happy with that plan. We can follow the advice of Abraham Zaleznik, psychoanalyst and Harvard Business School professor, who recommends that managers prioritize and delegate work in order to free up an hour at the end of the day, maybe not every day, but three out of five days a week. When we put the emphasis on working more effectively instead of "doing time" at the office, we give ourselves a chance for family recreation and intimacy on a daily basis, rather than always promising ourselves time to play later on.

PHASE ONE: CHANGE YOUR OWN ATTITUDE

Living a more balanced life-style makes ultimate good sense for you and your employees. Once you no longer abuse, misuse, or simply neglect your body's health, you in essence stop beating up on yourself. You give yourself a chance to deliver peak personal performances and the right to make wellness a priority within your work group. Still, as you know by now, before you can make dramatic outward changes, you have to change your attitude about the importance of maintaining your mental and physical health. Begin that internal shift now by walking through the CHANGING Process with me.

C CREATE A CONCRETE DESCRIPTION OF THE DESIRED CHANGE.

A good way to determine how you feel about yourself is to check the way you feel about your body. How do you treat it? What is your life-style?

_____

Lucky me, I look fit. Whether I eat a lot or a little, my weight stays at a healthy 135 pounds, which is slim when spread over my 5′10″. This is both good news and bad news. The good news is that it's hard for anyone but me to notice the increasing "tubbiness" around my waistline. The bad news is that because my slenderness hides so many sins, I'm not motivated to take care of my body.

Oh, I eat sensibly, have never smoked, and rarely drink. These are easy habits for me to maintain. My first book was about health, and with the exception of a mild craving for desserts, I eat sensibly every day. I've also meditated daily for over ten years. This helps me handle my stress quite well, so I don't feel the pressing need for exercise that people experience who have no regular way to release stress. But I'm inclined to ignore the stress-alleviating benefits of exercise. I'm chronically tired but too busy to waste seven or eight hours a night on sleep. Also, I don't feel good about how my body looks—especially when summertime rolls around and I don a bathing suit.

Periodically I get this creepy feeling that I'm going to burn up my body at an early age. I push it too hard and don't give it much time off. Play for me means writing an article or perhaps enjoying dinner and good conversation with a friend—not tennis or jogging or skiing. I figured out that in the last five years I have spent a total of 100 hours exercising—and that includes eight days of hiking on several backpacking trips. Overall that's not much exercise for an executive who would like to keep a healthy, trim body for another thirty to forty years.

H   HONESTLY EXAMINE YOUR MOTIVATION TO CHANGE.

Changing a habit is never easy. Are you serious about changing your life-style? Why are you troubling yourself to make the attempt?

I must admit that, for me, personal growth, work, and loving my daughter all have priority over exercising and sleeping enough. And yet I know that everything else would also improve if I took better care of my body. It does, after all, allow me to be alive and working. I guess I would say, then, that I'm moderately motivated—particularly if I can find a way to exercise and sleep more without cutting into my time with my daughter.

A ABANDON THE OLD BEHAVIOR IN YOUR IMAGINATION.

Allow yourself to imagine what life would be like for you if you no longer overworked (except for the occasional crisis) and in general led a more balanced life-style.

This was a bit difficult for me. I have never exercised regularly or routinely slept over six hours a night as an adult. Throughout high school and college I did floor exercises every day, and once, when I was thirty and recently divorced, I did yoga exercises each night for about a year so I could sleep better.

With such a limited history of exercising and sleeping, it was hard to imagine my life running smoothly and, at the same time, exercising regularly and sleeping seven to eight hours a night. I already lead a packed life. I'm like the smoker who stops smoking every year for a month or two and then picks it up again. I frequently made a pact to exercise regularly, did it for one to three months, and then dropped it until a year or more passed and I once again felt bad about my body.

The challenge here was to imagine myself exercising regularly over the entire course of my life—and liking it. I imagined that by exercising regularly I'd have more energy, be more productive, and therefore have more time to relax and sleep at the end of the day. But it was clear that I would continue only if the exercise felt good to do, if it became addictive in a healthy sort of way, and didn't get in the way of the other parts of my life (namely working and mothering) that were higher priorities.

I decided on swimming as my favorite exercise, so I imagined myself swimming three times a week and loving the way it felt to stretch my body, to glide through the water, to feel tension float away. Then I imagined that as the winter began to move in, I experimented on the gym equipment and found a personal routine that was really fun, plus a companion who liked exercising with me.

I saw all of this occurring during my lunch hour. In my imagination I saw that I would have the time three times a week, every week, to spend an hour working out at a nearby sports club. I saw myself being more productive in the afternoon and early evening hours, leaving me with time for a good seven hours of sleep each night.

N NAME THE CHANGE POSITIVELY.

Envision the changed you, revitalized by this new way of treating your body. Then put that vision into words and post it in a handy spot to remind you of your new goal.

For me, the statement was, "I thrive on regular exercise and plenty of sleep each night. A balanced life-style renews my energy and enthusiasm at work."

G GIVE ATTENTION TO PAYOFFS.

You got hooked on your present life-style because it gratified you in some way. What were those payoffs? Do they still satisfy you today? This step is frequently an eye-opener because what was once an important benefit may not seem so important now that you think about it.

One payoff that I noticed was the positive attention I got from my work successes. I also got a lot of love from my daughter when I was with her. But I got nothing from exercising and sleeping. No one noticed. I didn't look any different. No one that knows and cares about me thinks it's something I particularly need to do.

Another payoff was a bit more tangled. I had never let go of my adolescent picture of myself as a string bean. This androgynous view of myself, though outdated, permitted me to be pals with the men and women where I work. I have never been a competitor or a predator.

I IMAGINE THE PAST AND SEE HOW YOU BEHAVED.

Look at the beliefs that were operating in the past and how they affected what you did. Don't stop at two or three experiences. Try to recall five or ten different memories in the hope you'll recognize a pattern of behavior. Then relive those experiences, only this time imagine the new you in operation, enjoying and using your healthy body.

As far back as I can remember, I've much preferred thinking to doing. As a young child on our ranch, I sat in a tree and made up short stories rather than romp with my brother and male cousins, who were busy looking for arrowheads, chasing after cattle, and hunting deer.

In the fourth grade, I was one of the tallest in my class and therefore one of the fastest runners. That year I began having "stitches" in my side whenever I ran. The boys told me to breathe deeper and the stitches would go away. Well, that hurt, and I wasn't interested in hurting, so what I did instead was to run slower. I was, after all, more interested in being popular and having good grades than in being a good runner.

Later, in junior high school, I played on the basketball team and I had a similar set of experiences with my ankles. They were easily twisted and taping them was uncomfortable. So after a while, I became the scorekeeper rather than suffering a little physical discomfort. In high school I was a twirler and drum majorette for three years. This was more fun, more like dancing, which I always loved. But how I hated the marching practices in the Texas heat. My senior year, I was selected to perform on television with a jazz dance troupe. I was excited at first, but my friends thought the routine was a bit weird for South Texas. In the end, I didn't get much positive reinforcement from my "big opportunity."

As I looked at this past history of my life as a physical body, I felt a little sad. It was as if I hadn't taken much pleasure in the physical side of life. I'd always concentrated far more on mental and emotional activities, work and friends. Now I better understood why swimming and yoga appealed to me. Both are gentle and peaceful. Neither worked up a sweat.

When I sorted through those memories again, I imagined the new me in place. I saw myself first in the fourth grade, continuing to run even though it hurt. I saw myself loving to run very fast. Then I imagined that I made the high school track team, though in those days, at small country high schools, there was no girls' track. Still, this was okay in my imagination, right? I also saw myself absolutely loving to swim. I was a good swimmer even before I started school, and I saw myself continuing this and participating in the swim team, another luxury that our country school didn't have. Finally, I saw myself getting signed up for jazz dance classes in college. I had loved dancing all through school, and I was willing to commit myself to the daily "tortuous exercises" in order to allow my body this opportunity to express some of my deeper feelings. I continued to see myself move into young adulthood and then across the age forty boundary into middle age, all the while cherishing my body and treating it well by exercising it and keeping it tuned up.

N   NAIL DOWN THE NEW BEHAVIOR BY
USING MENTAL REHEARSAL.

How are you going to react to temptation in the future? Will you persist in exercising? Push yourself away from the table after one plateful? Shun the cocktail hour? Imagine how people will react to your new regimen. Here a word of caution is in order: Everyone will not applaud your new habits. When you give up candy, for example, the folks who stop at the candy machine regularly may feel threatened. Your shift toward wellness puts implicit pressure on them, making them uncomfortable. They're likely to feel it's better to pull you back down to their level.

I saw myself swimming at lunch and, in my imagination, I even heard a few people at work mention how relaxed I seemed and how good I looked. I imagined that all those hours of swimming and working out with weights improved my posture so that my shoulders lost their slump and my energy level soared. I saw myself walking into a room full of new people, knowing I looked great.

G   GRADUATE TO THE NEW BEHAVIOR.

Get your ego involved by letting your associates know about your new regimen. You won't want to backslide or fail with all those people looking on. Also, by letting your intentions be known, you become a role model throughout your organization.

I told the people I work with, those in the human resources department, the people in finance whose offices are near ours, and many of the line managers I regularly see, that I was swimming during lunchtime. I got some good-natured ribbing as a result. But then I was motivated more than ever to persist in exercising faithfully.

I kept swimming regularly, three times a week, and I began encouraging the people I knew best to do whatever they needed to do to get in good shape. We started a Weight Watchers group, initiated by my assistant Heidi Henderson, who got so revved up herself that she lost twenty pounds.

Lynne Forman, our employment manager, asked about a stress-management group, and that got going as another way of helping people handle stress better. Then we got a call from an employee requesting a quit-smoking program, in which the company paid part of the fees if the person stayed off cigarettes. All of this happened as we worked together, increasing our personal responsibility for staying healthy.

PHASE TWO: MANAGE TO SUPPORT THE MIND-BODY CONNECTION

No one is immune to trouble, though it does come in diverse forms. One person may be overweight, uptight, and out of shape. Another, bored with a job or lonely. Still another may have a terminally sick parent. Someone else may turn to alcohol to relieve stress.

Employees need help when personal affairs affect their productivity at work and when work problems spill over into their homes, making private lives as unhappy as work lives. All in all, this means that once you opt for a well body yourself, you will want to change your management style in ways that support the mind-body connection. Of course, you are a powerful role model to your employees. Your example of a life-style that balances work and play and provides mental and physical activities within your work community gives a strong orientation toward wellness. Let people see and hear of your successes, and you'll find willing followers in your move toward healthier ways of working.

STEP ONE: HELP EMPLOYEES ACHIEVE A BALANCE BETWEEN MENTAL AND PHYSICAL ACTIVITIES.

When employees begin to burn out on their jobs, they commonly try to work more and more. This phenomenon is reported by Dennis Jaffe and Cynthia Scott in *Take This Job and Love It.* Instead of seeking help, they cut themselves off from outside activities and relationships. Like a hamster on a treadmill, they keep on running without getting anywhere. They feel helpless, hopeless, and cut off from any source of serious help. To get off that treadmill rush toward burn-out, people need to connect with the information and people that can lend them a hand.

To keep your employees charged up, start some preventive programs of your own. Installing an information-dissemination program is well within your scope as a manager. You can route all sorts of articles around the office about diet, smoking, drinking, drugs, exercise, fitness, and their relationship to happiness, health, and even productivity. There are many such articles in the press today. It takes only your awareness and your "FYI" on the top to insure that your employees take a look at them.

Encourage employee activities, especially those that are physical. Encourage your employees to take stretch breaks. You can do this simply by taking them yourself and talking about them. Don't only suggest that people band together for softball and basketball games after work or on weekends. Join them, too. This will give your employees exposure to a different, more sociable, and more relaxed you. They'll learn to like you, not just respect you. And you'll be modeling the value of playing hard along with working hard.

STEP TWO: HELP EMPLOYEES SOLIDIFY RELATIONSHIPS
AND FORM SUPPORT GROUPS.

Jaffee and Scott discovered that charged-up employees, unlike burn-out victims, maintain their friends and family relationships and engage in hobbies and activities that balance work and play. As a result, charged-up employees enjoy longer and happier lives. That's not all. They also do better at work. That was the conclusion of a comparative study of managers of Illinois Bell, made by Salvatore Maddi, University of Chicago psychologist, and Suzanne Kobasa, a psychologist from City

University of New York. The study, reported in *Psychology Today,* found that healthier people have more commitment, challenge, control, and connection in their lives than unhealthy people. They don't have smoother lives, necessarily. According to Maddi, they simply stay healthy because they hold a world view that allows them to transcend stressful circumstances.

Actually, a support group may be simply a team of two. A person really needs just one other person to trust and on whom to unburden concerns. Given that, the person can talk through the situation. As a result, he or she may see the problem evaporate or reduce in size, or see the problem in a new way. Like the difference between choking down a snail for lunch, or relishing escargot, sometimes a situation can be adjusted to if it's looked at from another perspective.

STEP THREE: HELP EMPLOYEES ACHIEVE A BALANCE
BETWEEN THEIR WORK AND HOME LIVES.

Share your own experiences with balancing success at work with a satisfying home life. When your priorities are in line and you honestly believe you can live a balanced life, let your employees know how you do it. Moreover, if you really believe that your best workers should have peaceful home lives, be sure they go home at a reasonable hour most evenings. This is not to say that at times they won't be working late. But their daily routine probably shouldn't include more than forty-five hours of work in a normal week.

When Accountemps of New York surveyed one hundred personnel executives from among 1,000 of the largest U.S. companies, 81 percent of the personnel people they interviewed believed a seven- to eight-hour day provided the greatest productivity. Only 13 percent thought that working more than eight hours a day was most productive. Studies have found that productivity drops precipitously after the sixth hour of work in a day. Again, this is not to say that, when rush projects or challenging periods of the quarter roll around, people shouldn't be working the fifty to sixty hours a week that are necessary. But if they work those hours for long, they'll either burn out or face problems at home that will consume their energy for months to come. Keep balance in your own life and help your employees do it, too.

PHASE THREE: INTRODUCE THE MIND-BODY CONNECTION THROUGHOUT THE COMPANY

A variety of employee problems aren't susceptible to your role modeling or advice. Some problems require professional intervention or more time and money to solve than you, as an individual manager, have available. Because of this, corporations that are serious about supporting the mind-body connection target a network of resources, services, and training activities.

Together, these resources offer help to every employee in the company. By providing connection, comfort, and compassion, these programs give people a lift that can mean the difference between burning out on work or turning on to work. When enough managers use the support services themselves, and talk about them, a wellness network can become a great joining of hands. It acknowledges everyone's worth to the company and inspires optimal performance.

STEP ONE: PROVIDE EMPLOYEES WITH HELP FROM AN EMPLOYEE ASSISTANCE PROGRAM WHEN THEIR THINKING AND FEELING SIDES ARE OUT OF BALANCE.

Most people are far more willing to seek help for physical pains than emotional ones. Yet the suffering is no less real and the effect on job performance is surely equal to that of physical illness and injury.

Employee Assistance Programs (EAPs) help people work through personal problems with their families, friends, and work associates. While each company's program may differ in detail, in general the programs offer positive problem-solving assistance by providing employee counseling services as part of the company's benefits package. Professional counselors are trained to identify stress, substance abuse, and emotional problems. On occasion, you may refer an employee with significant drug or alcohol abuse problems to an EAP program as a condition of continuing employment. Still, problems don't have to be job threatening to claim the attention of an EAP counselor. The hope is that early referral will catch a problem while it's easy to solve. In fact, employees can go on their own for help with problems ranging from handling a teenager to dealing with a tough supervisor. Whatever troubles employees is the concern of the EAP program.

Employees are less reluctant to take advantage of corporate counseling programs when they know managers use them, too. At KLA, nearly everyone in human resources uses the company's counseling program so they can share their experiences with managers and employees. You will need to encourage your employees in the same way. Expose yourself to some sort of counseling, perhaps focused on your own career growth or on your management style. In just three or four sessions, you'll see that going to a counselor is quite different from your misconceptions about talking to a "shrink." Then talk to your fellow managers and your employees about the experience. Urge them to take the opportunity to do something that's good for them and to take responsibility for their own problems. In this way, you'll help them feel all right about going for help when they need it.

Gay Hendricks, a psychologist and executive consultant in Colorado Springs, Colorado, says that executives need their own EAP programs to overcome the tendency to deny problems. Paul Sherman, former director of the Alcoholism and Behavioral-Medical Programs of ITT Corporation and now president of his own EAP group, believes that all executives should be "obligated to spend a certain number of hours a year with the consultant to help deal with stress, family issues, problems with their employees, and examine concerns before they get larger."

Services such as flex-time, child care, sabbaticals, and information exchanges treat employees as capable adults eager to resolve conflicts once they have the information and resources to do so. Phoenix Mutual Life Insurance Company of Hartford, Connecticut, offers workshops to employees on handling the stress of being a working parent and finding quality child care. For employees' latchkey children, the company offers a five-session seminar to the children themselves. If you have an employee who needs reliable child care to assure a steady attendance record, your job is to inform the employee of available services and, where none exist, endeavor to get them developed.

Flex-time, for example, helps employees who are consistently late or don't get to work at all because of transportation, health, or child-care problems. By letting employees come in to work later or earlier than usual, flex-time shows the company trusts employees to work the number of hours they're paid for and relinquishes control over when they put in those hours. Among companies that use flex-time, researchers found that in 84 percent of the cases it reduced employee tardiness, in 75 percent of the cases it reduced turnover, and in almost 50 percent of the cases it increased productivity.

It's no wonder. Flex-time helps employees better balance work and home responsibilities before they become critical to the point of impacting performance. Whether it's used at an employee's discretion to make adjustments for doctor's appointments and other occasional but necessary interruptions in the workday, or to establish a more workable daily schedule, flex-time provides a way to relieve unnecessary stress.

Child care conflicts cause working parents to lose an average of eight working days a year. When old arrangements fail, parents need approximately ten hours to make new ones and, of course, most of those hours fall within the workday. Assistance in child care is provided by over 2,000 corporations, up from 700 three years ago.

The need grows daily. Mothers of children under three years of age are now the fastest-growing portion of the work force. Moreover, it's expected that by 1990 over 70 percent of all working women will have children. Since at least one out of every two employees will be a working parent, women aren't alone in needing child care services. Ten percent of participants at child care seminars at Bankers Trust of New York are men. Already, at the Wang Laboratories Child Care Center, over 40 percent of the employees who use the services are fathers. Stephen Segal, president of Resources for Parents at Work in Philadelphia, says, "Just as role definitions are becoming blurred in the workplace, so they are also broadening at home." With nuclear families the rule, a grandparent is rarely available, and a nanny is expensive and intrusive in a small city dwelling. Companies that provide reliable child-care services, within the company or shared by other companies, for general day care and for "sick child" day care, reduce absenteeism, turnover, and employee anxiety.

Sabbaticals help long-time employees take a well-earned break from routine to rejuvenate themselves. About one in ten major corporations offer these extended job absences that last from a month to a year. The breaks serve to counteract stress, provide time for travel and advanced study, and allow employees to return to work with a fresh point of view. At KLA, we provide a sabbatical of sorts in our anniversary trip program. All KLA employees who reach their sixth and twelfth anniversary dates are given funds to take a dream trip. These trips are budgeted to include an entire week for the employee plus a family member or significant other.

Job restructuring is offered in some companies to boost lagging interest or to decrease stress in work. Employees are cross-trained to permit them to rotate, transfer, or expand their responsibilities. Workers become more valuable as well as more satisfied. In low-growth companies, job restructuring prepares plateaued workers for transfer rather than layoff when business is down. In high-growth companies like KLA, it prepares people for promotion. In all companies, job restructuring permits responsibilities to be increased or decreased to match the individual's ability to cope.

STEP THREE: DEVELOP COMPANY INFORMATION EXCHANGES
THAT GIVE EMPLOYEES USEFUL INFORMATION
RELATED TO WORK AND FAMILY.

Company information exchanges provide employees with useful information and skills related to work and family. With 21.5 million women working today who have children under the age of eighteen, the topics covered in company programs are more important than ever. Few men or women have the luxury of concentrating on just a job or just raising children. They must do both, frequently without any help other than what their company provides.

At KLA, we offer informal "brown bag" lunch programs during work hours. We invite professionals to cover topics such as balancing time and commitments to work and family, stress management, parenting, and personal budgeting, since money is a frequent source of family arguments. These one- and two-hour programs end up costing us only $100 to $200 each. If your employees are as enthusiastic about the programs as ours at KLA, you can be sure it's well worth the time and money for the solid information, morale building, and community feelings they engender.

Some companies favor information exchanges on a bigger scale. While she was working as a benefits specialist at Monolithic Memories (now a division of Advanced Micro Devices) in Santa Clara, California, Toni Herald set up a wellness and health fair for its 3,000 employees. Digital Equipment Corporation has produced two work and family fairs for 2,300 employees, at two of its facilities, for a cost of about $700 each. The fairs provided information, a panel discussion, and films to employees who could stop by throughout the day. Regardless of a program's scale, large or small, the intent is to build skills and morale in people who must cope and want to excel as parents and employees.

STEP FOUR: PROVIDE FACILITIES, ACTIVITIES, AND TRAINING THAT STRENGTHEN THE MIND-BODY CONNECTION.

Facilities and activities can range from the simple to the sophisticated. Ardent Computer, in Sunnyvale, California, provides its employees with fresh popcorn out of professional popping machines. KLA serves mid-morning refreshments every Monday in the company cafeteria as a way of pulling people together and introducing new employees. We also have a volleyball court set up next to our building and Silicon Graphics has a basketball court. These are a common sight at many Silicon Valley companies. Because they are convenient and free, these games attract a crowd at lunchtime almost every day.

Some companies have very elaborate facilities. Kellogg has a recreational center at its corporate headquarters and its Battle Creek plant. Employees use the exercise bikes, rowing machines, weight equipment, jogging track, and aerobics room from dawn to midnight. Rockwell International has set aside over fifty acres of land for recreational and health facilities in its seven California locations. Remember, though, that aerobics and yoga classes and short parcourses for runners require almost nothing in the way of facilities. KLA's parcourse is located on the grass strip between the roadway and the parking lot.

Training can range from physical fitness courses, including nutrition, aerobic exercise, weight control, and smoking cessation, to relaxation and stress management programs. IBM is so sold on the value of wellness courses, that it sponsors approximately 1,800 a year for its employees, their families, and retirees. At Illinois Bell, a fifteen-week course taught employees how to cope with problems by becoming "hardier." At Octel Communications, I was brought in by Philip Johnston, Director of Human Resources, to provide stress management training to all employees. Each person attended a general session that lasted nearly two hours, and then more than half signed up for follow-up sessions to focus on specific stress management skills that they needed to develop. Managers enrolled in the course noticed their anxiety and depression dropped along with the headaches and sleeplessness they often experienced.

A pilot program at the General Motors plant in Fremont, California, allowed organizational psychologist David Frew to study the effects of Transcendental Meditation on 500 workers. He found their job satisfaction, performance, and personal relationships improved. Students of TM claimed they needed less sleep, drank fewer alcoholic beverages, and used less tobacco, aspirin, and coffee after they went through the program. At least half of the group found that they fell asleep faster, had a better ability to organize, felt more confident, and had more emotional stability than before. Prominent managers who meditate include Stanley Goodman, retired chairman of the May department stores; Mitch Kapor, founder of Lotus Development Corporation; George Troutman, vice president of Bell Helicopter; and Donald Weber, chairman of Financial Guardian Group.

Put good health and a balanced life-style on your priority list where it belongs. A balanced life-style for you and your employees is fundamental to creating and maintaining a personal sense of well-being. Then, share your feelings of being productive and satisfied. Where the mind-body connection remains unacknowledged, everyone suffers, even the stockholder. Where the mind-body connection is recognized and supported, the Worth Ethic thrives and so does the organization.

10

THE BIG WIN
Caring Pays Off for Companies

*"The life of wisdom must be a life of
contemplation combined with action."*
—M. SCOTT PECK, *The Road Less Traveled*

The Worth Ethic concept is elegantly simple. When you
feel good about yourself, you perform well. The greater your
feelings of self-worth, the better you perform. The better
you feel and the better you perform, the higher your expectations soar. It's a self-fulfilling prophecy.

But the Worth Ethic fulfills another prophecy as well.
Working from the inside out, once you feel good about yourself, you are free to appreciate other people's efforts and affirm
their personal value. That lets employees feel good about
themselves. They perform well. This makes you look good.
The company profits. Everyone wins.

The only thing standing between you and this inspiring
scenario is that profound change you need to make: You must
become keenly aware of your feeling side. Instead of being
satisfied with just thinking your way through life, you need to
be aware of how your body responds to life, too. How do you
feel about yourself, what you do at work, and the people you

work with there? You've been operating, up to now, on about four sticky cylinders. I want you to operate on all eight. Or all twelve, for that matter, if you're the V-12 Jaguar type. I want you to bring your heart to work. That means you need to feel, which requires changing at a very deep level, from the inside out.

Over the past decade, training has had a heavy emphasis on what is called behavioral modeling. People watch video tapes or demonstrations. They see somebody do something in a particular way, such as give useful feedback to a worker or do a performance evaluation. They are supposed to practice two or three times, do some role playing, and then actually make the change. Sort of, "Monkey see, monkey do."

In reality, as nearly every corporate trainer will tell you, many behavioral changes that are inspired by group training programs do not stick. Undoubtedly you've attended courses that proposed to teach you new ways to manage your time, command respect, ensure quality decision making, or organize projects to timely conclusion. The ideas sounded good. You tried them out. That's where you found new ideas are as easy to assume as a new title, as easy to shrug off as an old coat, and as easy to toss away as throwing in a bad poker hand. Genuine changes in the attitudes that control your behavior begin internally. Still, changing from the inside out isn't an easy thing to do.

OBSTACLES TO SUCCESS

You face three obstacles to success in adopting and supporting the Worth Ethic: substituting manipulation for real change, lacking discipline and dedication in your efforts, and failing to deal with potential resentment.

YOU SUBSTITUTE MANIPULATION FOR REAL CHANGE.

Because change isn't easy, you may think you'll just skip the CHANGING Process altogether. You may think you can achieve the "W. E." that's fundamental to the Worth Ethic without really changing inside all that much. But if you give way to temptation and use the Worth Ethic's psychological approach without changing inside, you will fail.

Suppose, for example, that you try to take Tom Peters's excellent advice to "catch somebody doing something right." Put that intention on your weekly "to do" list and then, Thursday afternoon about five o'clock, begin to wander the halls of your building looking for someone to praise. What's going to happen? Maybe you'll find a young woman engineer surrounded by piles of work, obviously settled in to work late into the evening, and you'll say, "That's dedication. You're a great employee," or something like that.

How will this employee react? That depends. If she has worked late several times this week, and is in sore need of some recognition, she may smile. She may feel the load's a little lighter because you notice her efforts. But suppose she's worked weekends and every evening for the past month. Suppose she's seen you leave promptly at 5:30 P.M. every afternoon. Suppose she thinks that, just once, it would be nice if you rescheduled a deadline or stayed late yourself and offered a bit of help. In that case, she may lean away from you with a perplexed frown on her face, and register her disbelief. She may even respond with a dry, "Sure, Bob." In other words, she may be suspicious and distrust your motives.

Why is that? Because your words don't match your actions. You're no real help, therefore your words sound insincere. Without an internal change, you're the same old person. You are operating from your logical side, not connecting with your feelings or the other person's. You are probably an action-oriented person, most managers are, and when you go through the motions without putting your heart into it, you leave a person feeling manipulated and used. "Change from the inside out" is the first requirement of the Worth Ethic. In *Management*, Peter Drucker warns that controlling and manipulating others is a " . . . self-destructive abuse of knowledge." Ultimately, you hurt yourself as well as your employee when you say the right words and use the right techniques without matching them to honest feelings and intentions.

We've all known and loved autocratic bosses who bark out orders yet have their hearts in the right place. They may yell, but we can count on them to be straight with us. We get irritated at their style, of course, but we know they value us, and they evoke our loyalty. It's better to ignore the psychological techniques than the internal changes. Drucker says, ". . . any manager, no matter how many psychology seminars he has attended, who attempts to put psychological despotism into practice will very rapidly become its first casualty. He will immediately blunder. He will impair performance. The work relationship has to be based on mutual respect."

Paul H. Schurr of the State University of New York at Albany, a leading researcher in how trust is built and used in business, has developed guidelines for deciding when, where, and how to trust someone else. His standards suggest how you can inspire others to trust you: Be sure your words and behavior are consistent, predictable, and dependable. Exchange information freely. Express your need for trust openly. Be realistic about your faith in others. Situations and people change. Giving trust only when it is justified reflects your own high standards of trustworthiness.

As a manager you try to influence others. Because you are able to see the broad picture, you can often foresee problems and forestall them if you succeed in influencing a team's approach to a task. Your job, as Drucker says, is "to make worker and working achieving." By manipulating, your attention is on your own interests. You are pretending you care about employees' welfare and needs to get a particular output from them. In contrast, when you manage by influencing, your intention is not solely to meet your own objectives, it's to help people get the work done. When you deal with people from the heart, you are working together to achieve what's good for the total work group. Your intention and your demands on yourself make all the difference.

YOU LACK DISCIPLINE AND DEDICATION IN YOUR EFFORTS.

It takes time to build your introspective muscles, patience to think back over your life, and courage to admit the truth about yourself and the past events that shaped your attitudes. You have to expect a lapse or two. We've all had the experience of making a resolution—maybe to cut out desserts—and we go along just fine for a while, then suddenly we go on a binge, eating a handful of candy or three pieces of pie.

Often change is stressful. Small wonder, then, that you may agree with the Worth Ethic in principle, yet find yourself saying, "Yes, but"—it's a great idea, but it just won't work. That attitude is typical of people who want to block their own change. If you are afraid to try, you can always find a reason why something won't work.

Besides, it's easier on the ego not to try at all than to try and then fail. Consider how you felt when you tried to quit smoking or tried to go on a diet. Think about the exercise you vowed you'd get but never did. It's natural to avoid an activity that is likely to fail and further destroy your fragile feelings of self-worth.

Yes, changing can inflict considerable pain. It demands honesty with yourself and then with your friends, your spouse, and your employees. It takes time. And patience. Still, it's rather like having the chance to live your life over, but this time you get to pick your parents and your sisters and brothers. With your dedicated efforts, your self-worth will be reborn and reinvigorated. Most people are more than willing to work hard at what they love. What I'm asking is that, this time, you invest in yourself. Admit you are worth loving. Be willing to work hard on yourself.

YOU FAIL TO DEAL WITH POTENTIAL RESENTMENT.

A word of warning. As you gain self-awareness, you'll begin to notice that your feelings about those around you aren't always positive. You'll be disappointed and maybe frustrated by people who concentrate exclusively on what they are thinking. You m: / be angry at them as well. You may wonder what good it does for you to empower others to grab all the glory. Your competitive-oriented old self will get discouraged, forgetting that glory, like love, is limitless. Take these feelings of discontent as good signs of your personal development. You are in the process of switching over to a long-term view of managing. Now's the time to reach out to the support network you will create by bringing your heart to work.

Have you seriously considered how people around you will interpret your efforts to relate to your emotional self as well as your logical self? Are you willing to suffer the consequences of change? You need to be prepared for the implications. People are going to notice that you are different. They will find you less predictable and therefore harder to manage and manipulate.

People rely on the predictability of others' behavior. If you change without warning, there's little likelihood that they'll understand what's going on. Unless you tell them to expect some changes in you, they will interpret these changes as manipulation. The very people you are counting on to support you will end up trying to pull you back to the way you have always been. After all, they may not like you now, but they long ago learned to cope with you the way you are.

Often the issues we most need to work on in our work lives are also getting in the way of optimal relationships at home. If this is true for you, you may find that you can look simultaneously at patterns in your home relationships that need work. You can clean it all up at one time—but be prepared for resentment on both fronts.

Your family may rebel. Roger Stockton, a senior vice president I once counseled through a career change, told me that his wife Maggie's reaction to his shift in attitudes totally surprised him. Originally Maggie was the emotional switch within the family, buffering the anger between himself and the kids and the rivalries between the younger and older child. As

Roger gained skill at noticing and reacting honestly to other people's feelings, he became more expressive, and the emotional buffering his wife provided wasn't so necessary any more. The children began to come directly to him. He liked this new closeness with them, even though the encounters were sometimes heated and time-consuming. Then one day Maggie burst into tears and, after some prompting, admitted she felt excluded and even somewhat jealous of his new relationship with the children. She'd seen her own source of meaning in life eroding and didn't like it.

The same feelings of resentment and jealousy can arise in secretaries and administrative assistants as well. They will see their role as intermediary evaporating, once managers can handle emotional issues on their own. In fact, everyone you deal with at work may react in ways you didn't expect. So you will need to develop strategies for approaching the people you have a lot of contact with, either at home or at work.

Talk with your family members, all your direct reports, your manager, and any other people with whom you come into close contact. Where you are comfortable doing so, share with them some of the insights you are after and the shifts in attitude and style you hope to make. In all cases, let them know you are planning some changes and warn them that they'll be seeing shifts in you in the near future. They should expect to see you displaying new levels of self-awareness, being more introspective, and making growth leaps.

BUILD INTROSPECTIVE SKILLS

Introspection is the major skill necessary to change yourself. Without it, you'll never be able to experience your own worth. Some people seem to have innate self-understanding (my daughter, Catherine, is such a person). Some people struggle to achieve skill in this area. It takes a lot of practice for them to connect with what's happening inside themselves and then to make deep connections with others.

Everybody finds certain tasks particularly grueling. For me, it's exercise. I need a very structured support system to keep me on an exercise program. Likewise, if you have trouble developing introspective skills on your own, you may want to seek outside help. Two reliable types of resources are the individual management consultant or clinical psychologist, and the community center or church growth program.

To select a management consultant or psychologist to work with, look first at that person's level of empathy and ability to promote personal insight. You don't need someone who is especially good at thinking through strategic plans. You need someone with the right chemistry. Personal chemistry is a difficult thing to define, but easy to recognize. It's the feeling you had when you chose your first "steady" in high school, your first car, and your first $400 suit. As one teenager put it, "She's great because she thinks I'm great." It's essentially a choice made on how the person makes you feel about yourself.

That's not to say you shouldn't look at objective differences. This person should have some kind of credentials that tell you he or she is skilled at facilitating an internal change. Typically, this means the person has at least a master's degree in psychology. The person should have some years of experience as a management consultant or clinical counseling experience as a psychologist, working with people individually and in small groups, to help them solve problems from the inside out. The person should also display a good balance between thinking and feeling.

Interview the management consultant or psychologist carefully. Ask specifically what changes this person has facilitated in other people and the approach used to produce those changes. Ask for examples of two or three others who had some of the same problems you have and how those problems were handled. Ask what the consultant did, how long it took, and what the manager did to make the process a success.

Finally, ask the reverse. Say that you realize that this kind of consulting is not like plastic surgery. You don't expect this person to give you an anesthetic and do something that will change you dramatically in a few hours' time. You know that the kinds of changes you are talking about require your cooperation and support. Clearly, then, there are plenty of people who are too resistant or haven't the insight for these kinds of change. Ask if the consultant has worked with people like this. Ask what kinds of patterns the people had who didn't change. And follow up with any concerns you have about the type of person who didn't change, particularly if you are like that, too.

An in-depth interview tells you how you compare with other people the consultant or psychologist has worked with successfully in the past. Listen especially for the person's ability to think in terms of results. Be alert for the "soft stuff," such as being told the person was more open or more caring. You want to hear specifics. You want to learn, for example, that the manager built a more innovative organization because creative people began to love working there. You want to hear that the person you are working with will help you produce a significant, observable difference in how well you acknowledge your own worth and the worth of others.

Many church organizations and community centers offer marriage encounter and couples programs that help people develop self-awareness and relationship skills. While these programs focus on personal growth and family problems, you already know how the issues that get in the way of relationships in one part of your life also impact your ability to relate effectively in the other. Whatever you learn in these programs can be used in the office or manufacturing plant as well. There's one special advantage to working on improving relationships at home: You begin to create your support network.

BUILD A SUPPORT NETWORK

At this point, what you need is a strong friendship with someone. Women have historically confided in close friends and they are often quite good at these kinds of relationships. Men, on the other hand, are less accustomed to seeking comfort from another person in all but the most overwhelming crises. If your spouse is also your good friend, choose your spouse as your confidant. Who better to turn to or practice on? On the other hand, if your spouse is not someone who can listen to you calmly and empathetically, choose a sympathetic work associate or perhaps even your manager.

If you are a man and are lucky enough to have a woman friend who is able to view you simply as another person, by all means choose her as a confidant. Many men seem to develop this kind of long-term friend when they are between marriages. Don't be overly concerned if you discover yourself developing some sexual feelings as a natural response to close friendship. It's just that, a natural response and one that doesn't have to be acted upon. Concentrate on your intention to gain empathetic support. While a close friend can't be expected to know the counseling techniques that will teach you to be introspective, that person can certainly give you practice and support at being self-disclosing.

Next, recruit someone else to change along with you. Begin, perhaps, with employees who are receptive to the same sort of journey. You'll find that most people are held back by their own psychological makeup, much as you are. If you give people an opportunity to join forces with you, you will see their feelings of self-worth, their connectedness, and their productivity at work go up along with your own. In addition, you will find that this kind of partnership encourages each person to accept the change in the other. You've shaped another loop in your support network.

MAKE CHANGING YOUR NUMBER ONE PRIORITY

Tom Peters reminds us, "Attention is all there is." To change from the inside out, you have to pay attention to yourself. You have to make changing your number one priority. That means you need some quality time.

Customarily, we have peace and quiet for perhaps five

minutes a day while we're in the shower and for half an hour or so while we're commuting. The business of changing requires time to reflect without distraction. You will need time alone, on long walks or slow jogs, or watching the sun rise, or simply sitting still somewhere. At first you will use this quality time for some self-talk. You will be thinking, because that's the way you've always operated in the past, but at least you will be thinking about how you feel. The possibility of recognizing your own self-worth lives in this vulnerable, softer side of who you are.

You may notice the bad feelings first and talk about them to yourself. Perhaps you feel very critical of yourself and others, so you will begin to think through the CHANGING Process and dredge up the memories of times past when someone else was highly critical of you. Maybe you feel pigeonholed or overworked in your present job. Are you angry or discouraged? The fact that you are noticing your feelings is a good beginning.

Ten or twenty years ago, you buried your emotions inside and didn't let them out. Now you have the confidence of a successful adult. You can give yourself permission to notice how your body responds to life. When you feel angry, do you get a fleeting headache or pain in your stomach? When you feel contented, are you warm inside and glowing on the outside?

It's time to admit that you're not half bad. As a matter of fact, you're a pretty good person and worth a lot more than most people give you credit for. Now that you've led yourself through the CHANGING Process in the preceding chapters, you know yourself better and probably like yourself a lot more.

LOOK FOR THE WORTH ETHIC

You will see your company with new eyes as you make a commitment to the Worth Ethic. You will appreciate the company that gives you the psychological space in which to change and grow. You will chafe at the restrictions of an inflexible, overstructured company.

I admitted, from the very beginning, that I deliberately sought out a perfect opportunity to introduce the Worth Ethic where I worked. I feel extremely lucky to have found KLA. If your company is unlikely to support the Worth Ethic, at least in your lifetime, you may have to "vote with your feet" and move to a new company.

Some basic library research and a series of interviews will tell you if you've found a company that's open to the Worth Ethic values. Look for articles about the company and its senior management group. What does the company produce? What kinds of services does it provide? Technical companies tend to be younger and have more members of the new work force. Who sits in the senior management group? If the average age of this group is much past fifty, they will be unaware of the Worth Ethic forces at work in the new work force. That doesn't mean you can't lead them to change, but it will take time.

Insist on a series of interviews. Make contact with as many people as possible throughout the company. To what extent is the Worth Ethic already in place? Ask the hard questions, ones that call for stories. Don't ask, "Is this an innovative company?" Ask instead, "What innovative ideas have you implemented that were resisted at first?" Give your interviewer permission to answer negatively. Admit that everyone has to operate in gray ethical areas, and then ask, "What ethical dilemmas have you faced and how did you solve them?"

Ask for specifics, such as, "How did you recognize someone's good performance this week?" If no answer is forthcoming, you know that company isn't high on praise. Find out what innovative projects your prospective manager approved in the past six months and get him to explain the approval process. If a long time passed from initial idea to eventual funding, you are probably considering a move to a bureaucracy.

Stop by the company cafeteria and ask an employee, "How hard is it for you personally to balance your home and work life?" Ask, too, "If you did a superb job on a project, what sort of recognition would you expect to get from that effort?"

THE WORTH ETHIC WORKS

Wherever you work over the next decade, you face quite a risk. You're going to be in the same situation as Noah when God ordered him to build a mighty ark. Noah believed that a big rain was coming, but a lot of people made fun of him as he wielded his hammer and loaded his animals. He took quite a chance. What if his ark building hadn't been followed by a significant rainfall?

You face the same risk and the same opportunity to keep things afloat in the next century. The new workers are different from the "work ethic" workers of the past, and like Noah, you face two alternatives. Noah could hope that he was facing an ordinary heavy rain, one that would pass in a day or so, or he could prepare for a forty-day-and-forty-nighter that would change the total terrain of the world. You face a crisis of competitiveness. You can hope that what you've been hearing isn't true or you can make the paradigm shift from adversary to collaborator with the new work force.

Maybe you aren't a president of a multimillion-dollar-a-year company. Maybe you aren't even a manager. But whatever your title and job responsibilities, you have the power to bring your heart to work. You can boost your personal satisfaction with life in general and with your work in particular. And that's not all—you can help your employees bring their hearts to work, too. You can nurture them as they strive for personal growth and professional advancement themselves. You can encourage them to use their creativity to make a difference in their jobs. You can lead their efforts to find meaning in work.

When you do, prepare to applaud your successes. Your own work group and your company will be more successful when employees stop wasting one-third of their workday and tap into their unused capabilities. As the Worth Ethic way of working becomes ingrained, you'll find work's a more fluid, relaxed, enjoyable place to be. With the Worth Ethic in place, calling forth the best efforts of people's minds, bodies, and hearts to create worthy goods and services, there will be so much self-worth in action, so much value produced because people feel good about themselves, that everyone who works with you is going to feel you've had a grand and glorious big win.

Celebrate that success in a big way. After all, there will be more profits to spend. The Worth Ethic works.